Aaron Renn was one of the first evangelicals to understand the crisis facing all Christians committed to living out biblical orthodoxy in these post-Christian times. His insights guide me in my own thinking about fidelity under fire. Aaron is fearless, Aaron is faithful—and Aaron is right about the harsh reality believers face. Neither wishfulness nor winsomeness is adequate to meet the challenges, and the full-throated rage that electrifies online Christian discussion feels good but accomplishes very little. *Life in the Negative World* is both a work of practical hope and a serious book for serious believers learning how to be strangers in a strange land.

ROD DREHER, AUTHOR OF *THE BENEDICT OPTION* AND *LIVE NOT BY LIES*

Rarely does one encounter a writer and analyst who can cut through the noise on Christianity and culture the way Aaron Renn does. His content is rich, analytical, insightful and comes from a place of authentic faith. Like the men of Issachar, Renn understands the times.

HUNTER BAKER, DEAN OF COLLEGE OF ARTS AND SCIENCES AND PROFESSOR OF POLITICAL SCIENCE, UNION UNIVERSITY

American Christians aren't used to living in a society hostile to our core beliefs. This book is a much-needed wake-up call. Renn lays out the challenges and gives sage advice about how to bear fruitful witness. A must-read for every Christian leader.

R. R. RENO, EDITOR OF *FIRST THINGS*

The most important distinction in the American church today is not the one between liberal and conservative, or high church and low church, or mainline and evangelical; no, the most important distinction in the American church today is between those who recognize that we live in the negative world and those who haven't yet accepted that fact. I am in the former camp, and Aaron Renn has given me the vocabulary I need to help others see the world as it is. Every now and then a writer and thinker comes along who helps us see the world more clearly, and Aaron Renn has been that guide for me. In *Life in the Negative World* he does two important things: (1) He helps us see the world as it actually is and not as we wish it to be. (2) He gives us a way forward. I'd recommend this book to every pastor I know, and I'd like everyone in my church to read it.

ANDREW FORREST, SENIOR PASTOR OF ASBURY
CHURCH, TULSA, OKLAHOMA

LIFE

IN THE

NEGATIVE
WORLD

LIFE

IN THE

NEGATIVE
WORLD

CONFRONTING CHALLENGES IN
AN ANTI-CHRISTIAN CULTURE

AARON M. RENN

ZONDERVAN REFLECTIVE

Life in the Negative World

Copyright © 2024 by Aaron M. Renn

Published in Grand Rapids, Michigan, by Zondervan. Zondervan is a registered trademark of The Zondervan Corporation, L.L.C., a wholly owned subsidiary of HarperCollins Christian Publishing, Inc.

Requests for information should be addressed to customercare@harpercollins.com.

Zondervan titles may be purchased in bulk for educational, business, fundraising, or sales promotional use. For information, please email SpecialMarkets@ Zondervan.com.

ISBN 978-0-310-15519-5 (audio)

Library of Congress Cataloging-in-Publication Data
Names: Renn, Aaron M., 1959- author.
Title: Life in the negative world : confronting challenges in an anti-Christian culture / Aaron M. Renn.
Description: Grand Rapids : Zondervan, 2024.
Identifiers: LCCN 2023031013 (print) | LCCN 2023031014 (ebook) | ISBN 9780310155157 (hardcover) | ISBN 9780310155171 (ebook)
Subjects: LCSH: Christianity and culture—United States. | United States—Church history—21st century. | BISAC: RELIGION / Christian Living / Social Issues | RELIGION / Religion, Politics & State
Classification: LCC BR115.C8 R435 2024 (print) | LCC BR115.C8 (ebook) | DDC 261.0973—dc23/eng/20230807
LC record available at https://lccn.loc.gov/2023031013
LC ebook record available at https://lccn.loc.gov/2023031014

Cover design: Gearbox Studio
Cover photo: © Betty Johnson / Alamy Stock Photos
Interior design: Sara Colley

Printed in the United States of America

23 24 25 26 27 LBC 5 4 3 2 1

To my wife, Katy

And to the many future generations of faithful Christians yet to come in America

CONTENTS

PART 4: ENGAGING MISSIONALLY

ACKNOWLEDGMENTS

I WOULD LIKE TO THANK SOME OF THE MANY PEOPLE who helped make this book possible, starting with my editor Ryan Pazdur and his entire team at Zondervan Reflective. I'd also like to thank my agent, Dan Balow, who ably marketed my proposal.

Thank you to R. R. Reno and *First Things* magazine for commissioning and publishing "The Three Worlds of Evangelicalism" article, and for being such great supporters of turning it into this book. I want to also specifically note James Wood, who suggested that *First Things* commission me to write that piece while he was an editor there.

I also benefited from the critics of my original article, who helped me reduce confusion and better frame some of my arguments in this version. And I profited from several people in my Member group of closest supporters who read and commented on early drafts of my manuscript.

None of this would be possible if not for those who have championed my writing on Christianity. Thank you to my many readers who have passed along and recommended my work over the years. I'd like to especially thank Rod Dreher, Douglas Wilson, and Mark Galli, who played a vital role in helping me reach a critical mass of readers. And also Mike Sugimoto, who, in passing along my original newsletter version of the three worlds framework to Dreher, made the difference between me continuing to write in this space and walking away from it.

My financial supporters also played a critical role in making this book happen. I'd like to especially thank Nate Fischer, Tom Owens, and Peter Morrison, who made it possible for me to venture full time into this space. I also could not do what I do without the many other people who financially support me by subscribing to my newsletter or joining my Member program. Thank you so much.

INTRODUCTION

IN 2014 THE BENHAM BROTHERS, JASON AND DAVID, were sitting on top of the world. The Benhams are the identical twin sons of an alcoholic bar owner turned pastor and noted pro-life activist. Raised as Christians, the brothers played baseball at Liberty University and were later drafted at the professional level. After their brief careers in the pros, they planned to go into traditional nonprofit ministry before realizing they had just as much opportunity to advance mission through for-profit work. They started a successful real estate company, which in turn led to a dream opportunity: the chance to have their very own home rehab television show on HGTV. The show was called *Flip It Forward*.[1]

This dream turned into a nightmare for Jason and David after activists attacked them for their Christian beliefs. Labeling them anti-Islam and anti-gay as well as anti-abortion, these groups pressured HGTV to drop the Benhams.[2] HGTV canceled their show in midproduction, even though the crew said the brothers were "extremely genuine, nice guys" and didn't push their religious beliefs.[3] The firestorm of controversy saw the Benhams and their show's cancellation featured across major media outlets: ABC, CBS, CNN, MSNBC, the *New Yorker*, TMZ, the *Hollywood Reporter*, and more.

In 2000 Dave Cover and his team planted the Crossing

church in Columbia, Missouri, home to the state's flagship University of Missouri. The church's name reflected the team's hope to build bridges to those who were not Christian, or who held negative stereotypes about the faith. Outreach to the community was one of their core values.

One way they did this was sponsoring a local film festival called True/False. While this was a secular festival, the church thought the films featured were asking the right questions about the human condition and what was wrong with the world. So though some people in both the festival organization and the church were initially apprehensive about working together, they decided to move forward.

The Crossing ultimately became one of the festival's biggest sponsors, and this unique and fruitful relationship between a Bible-believing evangelical church and a secular progressive film festival became nationally known. It was positively featured in the *New York Times*, which highlighted how the two groups were able to work together while disagreeing on some matters.[4]

Then in October 2019, a sermon at the Crossing affirmed that there are only two genders, saying, "Gender is not a social construct. Men and women are foundational to God's plan. God is not pleased when we blur genders."[5] This sermon caused a major controversy in the Columbia community. As the Crossing stood by their position, institutions in town came under pressure to drop partnerships with the church. The True/False Film Fest decided to do so, cutting ties. An art gallery in town did likewise.[6] A church that had worked hard never to offer gratuitous offense suddenly found itself a pariah in parts of the local community it had been trying to reach.

Though the Benham Brothers and the Crossing share an evangelical commitment to the gospel of Jesus Christ, their styles and strategies for taking it into the world were radically different. The Benhams came from a culture war background.

The Crossing was much more about cultural engagement. Yet both experienced the same fate at the hands of secular society. Regardless of their approach, the world wasn't willing to accept their beliefs.

The fact that Christians like these are at risk of being ostracized for their beliefs reveals that we've now entered a new and unprecedented era in America, one I call the "negative world." That is, for the first time in the history of our country, orthodox Christianity is viewed negatively by secular society, especially by its elite domains. This shift to the negative world poses a profound challenge to American evangelicals and their churches and institutions. It also helps to explain why there's been so much turmoil and conflict within the evangelical world and even why some believers have "deconstructed" their faith.

This book is about the shift to the negative world, what that means, and how to live in this new reality. I describe the shifts in the relationship between culture and Christianity over the past sixty years, tracing the fall of Christianity's status from being softly institutionalized in the 1950s to being increasingly seen as a threat to society's institutions today. I also examine the strategies evangelicals used to respond to the various phases of this decline and how those approaches have changed and even deformed under the new pressures of the negative world.

I argue that fresh strategies and approaches need to be developed to respond to the new and difficult challenges posed by the negative world. I don't pretend to have all the answers or to provide you with a detailed road map for what to do in the negative world. We're in a new territory where there is no map, and it's a constantly changing and evolving landscape. This means, then, that we will have to explore, to find a path through this new environment under conditions of uncertainty and discomfort.

I come at this problem from a unique perspective. I spent

nearly two decades in the technology and management consulting industry, primarily with the global firm Accenture, where I was what today would be called a managing director. In that career, I advised Fortune 500 companies on how to navigate the rapidly changing technology and business landscape. I then took my management consulting skills and applied them to the challenges facing America's urban areas. That led to a second career as an urban policy researcher and journalist in which I spent several years as a senior fellow at the Manhattan Institute, a think tank in New York. My insights have been featured in a wide range of national and global media outlets, including the *New York Times*, the *Guardian*, the *Wall Street Journal*, and the *Atlantic*.

I also have a personal background in very different parts of America and the evangelical world. I grew up in rural Southern Indiana, where I attended fundamentalist Pentecostal churches with a culture war orientation in the Assemblies of God denomination. As an adult, I've mostly lived in urban centers like Manhattan and Chicago, and I'm a Presbyterian who has attended churches with a cultural engagement approach. I thus have a foot in two of the evangelical camps that seem most in conflict today, and I think I have a good appreciation of both their strengths and limits.

Now I've combined these different parts of my background to focus on helping American evangelicals successfully adapt to the negative world in the twenty-first century. Management consultants and think tank researchers sit at the intersection of theory, practice, and journalism. We draw on theory as well as on our own research to help understand the world, then apply and communicate our findings in a compelling way. We create frameworks and tools to help people understand their environment and make decisions about how to act in it.

That's what I hope to do with this book as I provide a

framework of the "three worlds of evangelicalism"—the positive, neutral, and negative worlds—that I originally developed in 2014 and later published in the February 2022 print issue of *First Things*, an influential New York magazine about religion and the public square founded by Richard John Neuhaus. The framework describes the stages of decline of the status of Christianity in America over the past sixty years.

I also describe the three strategies evangelicals developed in response to this decline: culture war, seeker sensitivity, and cultural engagement. Then I provide a set of considerations and ideas for life in the negative world across three dimensions of evangelical life: personal, institutional, and missional. I talk about how to live as Christian individuals and families, how we should structure our churches and institutions, and how we can take advantage of the new opportunities the negative world will open up for mission and evangelism.

I don't, however, tell you or your church exactly what to do. Rather, I intend this set of ideas and inputs to be one you can use to make thoughtful and prayerful decisions for yourself. They aren't intended to be the last word on the negative world, but rather a starting point for further exploration.

I want to be clear that I am neither a pastor nor a theologian. I don't claim to be an authoritative Bible teacher—although with limited exceptions, I mostly avoid making arguments based on the Bible. And as an evangelical, I, of course, use Scripture to inform and illustrate my work. But this book is primarily in the genres of cultural analysis and strategy, where I do have significant professional experience. It's about the social, cultural, and political context in which pastors and theologians have to apply God's Word today. In keeping with my professional background in consulting and the think tank world, this book is also designed to be useful and practical rather than ivory tower academic or scholarly.

While *Life in the Negative World* may be useful for Roman Catholics or those from other Christian traditions, it's primarily written with evangelicals in mind. Defining what an evangelical is can be as difficult as trying to define jazz, and I use a sociological rather than a theological approach. The most common method for identifying religion in social science surveys divides Protestants into three main groups: Mainline, Evangelical, and Black Protestant.[7] I similarly classify any Protestant who is not mainline or from the black church tradition as an evangelical. I am intentionally casting a broad net in determining who is an evangelical.

Similar negative world trends also exist in other Western countries. For example, in 2022 in Australia, a highly qualified former banker and consultant was forced to resign just one day after being named the new president of a soccer club because people took offense at his church's teachings.[8] Because these trends are international, people outside America may also benefit from this book. But its focus is the United States, and I don't attempt to provide cultural diagnoses of foreign countries. Nor do I give contemporary foreign examples for American evangelicals to copy. That is for experts in those other countries to take on.

My focus is American evangelicals specifically. Non-evangelicals or non-Americans can benefit from much of what I share, but they'll need to adapt it to their own specific traditions and circumstances.

Whether or not you're an American evangelical, I hope this book helps you navigate the new world we find ourselves in—the negative world. Let's begin by looking at how we got here.

PART ONE

WELCOME

TO THE

NEGATIVE
WORLD

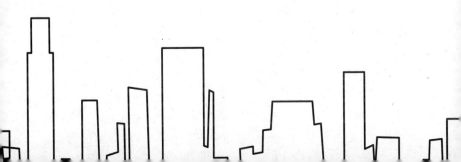

CHAPTER 1

THE THREE WORLDS OF EVANGELICALISM

AMERICAN CHURCH ATTENDANCE REACHED A HIGH-water mark during the 1950s, when around half of adults attended services on Sunday mornings.[1] In that era, going to church was just another part of being an upstanding member of society, like voting or volunteering. So perhaps not all the people in the pews were especially devout, but they were there. Christianity and church attendance had normative force in society.

The divisions in society then were primarily racial, ethnic, and sectarian (and also class, even though we Americans have never liked to think we have social classes). America historically had an Anglo-Protestant identity. Significant assimilation of Ellis Island–era immigrants by the 1950s had reduced the "Anglo" component of that, though without eliminating ethnic, to say nothing of racial, distinctions. Some described the midcentury period as the era of the "triple melting pot," best articulated in the title of Will Herberg's book *Protestant, Catholic, Jew*. We see this also in President Eisenhower's famous line, "Our form of government has no sense unless it is founded in a deeply felt religious faith, and I don't care what it is."[2] After being elected president, Eisenhower, who had not previously been a church member, was baptized and joined the Presbyterian Church.[3]

Even so, the Protestant component of American identity remained strong. Not just Christianity, but specifically Protestant Christianity was dominant; Protestants were still a two-thirds majority. Though diminished from its heyday, America still had a powerful upper-class WASP establishment: the White Anglo-Saxon Protestants. While the WASPs might compromise on the Anglo-Saxon part of their identity, Protestantism remained an upper-class boundary. Jews were blackballed (or subjected to a quota) in some institutions. Even Catholics were viewed as suspect. John F. Kennedy's election as the first Catholic president in 1960 was controversial precisely because of his religious background.[4]

America was thus a Christian, specifically Protestant, nation in some respects. That doesn't mean the country had an officially established religion or was always governed as a nation in line with Christian teachings or without serious injustices. But Christianity was publicly held in honor. It held normative force such that even many unbelievers attended church. And Christian moral and ethical teaching also had normative force. Just as men knew they should aspire to behave as gentlemen even when they failed to do so, people of that era understood that they should go to church, or at least seek to live up to Christian standards of behavior, even if they themselves weren't religious. They might have even suffered social consequences for not doing so.

Additionally, Christianity was a key component of American culture. Everyone from evangelists to politicians to writers was able to assume basic familiarity with Christianity and its themes. Consider how Christianity sits at the heart of James Baldwin's 1953 novel *Go Tell It on the Mountain*, for example.[5]

At this time, even the critiques of American injustice often took place within a Christian framework in keeping with the long history of reform movements in Christendom. Significant legal and social discrimination against blacks was pervasive in this era. Yet the critique of this injustice against black Americans drew from Christian arguments. Note the heavy participation of ministers like the Reverend Martin Luther King Jr. as leaders of the civil rights movement. King made frequent use of biblical argumentation to support his demands for justice. His famous "Letter from Birmingham Jail" was addressed to "My Dear Fellow Clergymen" and makes no sense without its Christian theological content.[6]

Russell Moore, now editor in chief of *Christianity Today* magazine, critically described that time in America this way:

> For much of the twentieth century, especially in the South and parts of the Midwest, one had to at least claim to be a Christian to be "normal." During the Cold War, that meant distinguishing oneself from atheistic Communism. At other times, it has meant seeing churchgoing as a way to be seen as a good parent, a good neighbor, and a regular person. It took courage to be an atheist, because explicit unbelief meant social marginalization. . . .
>
> In the Bible Belt of, say, the 1940s, there were people who didn't, for example, divorce, even though they wanted out of their marriages. In many of these cases, the motive wasn't obedience to Jesus' command on marriage but instead because they knew that a divorce would marginalize them from their communities.[7]

While, as Moore stressed, this era did not necessarily make everyone into a serious, devout Christian, it was a cultural environment structured to be friendly to Christianity, at least Protestant Christianity, and its ethical system.

Starting sometime in the 1960s—perhaps we could date the start of it to the assassination of President Kennedy in 1963, six months after King's Birmingham letter—this system began to break down. Social upheavals convulsed the country. Church attendance declined. Christian belief declined. People began questioning Christian moral teachings. Societal views of Christianity and the church changed as old truths were called into question. The overall status of Christianity in American society and its moral hold on the nation declined, portending radical shifts in the relationship between Christianity and the broader culture.

THE THREE WORLDS

Since that bygone midcentury era, the status of Christianity in America has passed through multiple thresholds as it declined, dividing that post-1963 period into three major eras, or worlds, characterized by three ways society at large has viewed and related to Christianity. These are the positive world, the neutral world, and the negative world (dates are approximate).

- **POSITIVE WORLD (1964–1994).** Society at large retains a mostly *positive* view of Christianity. To be known as a good, churchgoing man or woman remains part of being an upstanding citizen in society. Publicly being a Christian enhances social status. Christian moral norms are still the basic moral norms of society, and violating them can lead to negative consequences.
- **NEUTRAL WORLD (1994–2014).** Society takes a *neutral* stance toward Christianity. Christianity no longer has privileged status, but nor is it disfavored. Being publicly known as a Christian has neither a positive nor

a negative impact on social status.[8] Christianity is one valid option among many within a pluralistic, multicultural public square. Christian moral norms retain some residual effect.

- **NEGATIVE WORLD (2014–PRESENT).** In this era, society has an overall *negative* view of Christianity. Being known as a Christian is a social negative, particularly in the higher status domains of society. Christian morality is expressly repudiated and now seen as a threat to the public good and new public moral order. Holding to Christian moral views, publicly affirming the teachings of the Bible, or violating the new secular moral order can lead to negative consequences.

As the status of Christianity in America eroded, it passed through two tipping points: one from positive to neutral in the early 1990s, and the other from neutral to negative in the mid-2010s. The three different worlds were products of this general decline, though it wasn't a perfectly straight or smooth line.

Although I use the phrase *negative world*, it might be better to say Christianity is viewed suspiciously rather than negatively. Simply identifying as a Christian in this world can still be acceptable in society, though it may generate initial skepticism. But the contents of a person's Christian faith can't conflict with today's secular culture and ideologies. Someone who holds to thoroughly progressive beliefs politically and socially will not be rejected simply on account of professing a Christian faith or even regularly attending church. This is especially true if the person is in a denomination such as the Episcopal Church, which in the public mind is associated with political and social progressivism.[9]

But someone who holds to historic Christian beliefs will find himself in conflict with secular culture at several points.

This can and often does generate suspicion, negative reactions, or even hostility. Holding these beliefs or expressing them in any way is not acceptable in many elite domains of society, like the corporate world, academia, and the majority of the nonprofit sector. This aspect of the negative world, in which a denatured Christianity is acceptable but orthodox Christianity is not, pressures evangelicals to find ways to make their theological beliefs align with the ideologies of today's secular culture.

THREE WORLDS, THREE SCANDALS

The differences among these three worlds can be readily observed through the changes in cultural sexual ethics as seen in the following presidential sex scandals, one in each of the three worlds.

In the positive world of 1987, the *Miami Herald* reported that Colorado senator Gary Hart, a front-runner in the 1988 presidential race, had a young woman named Donna Rice stay overnight in his Washington town house when his wife wasn't there.[10] A media frenzy over Hart having a possible affair—and subsequent allegations—forced him to drop out of the race.

In the neutral world of 1998, the *Drudge Report* broke the story that President Bill Clinton had been having an affair with intern Monica Lewinsky, including engaging in sex acts adjacent to the Oval Office.[11] Clinton was badly damaged by the scandal but survived it as the Democratic Party rallied around him and publicly decided his private behavior wasn't relevant to his job.

In the negative world of 2016, Donald Trump, a man whose persona over a forty-year career in the public eye had been antithetical to Christian moral norms—exemplified by infidelity, boastfulness, and greed—was the Republican nominee for president and supported by several voting blocs of evangelical Christians. An attempt to derail his candidacy with an October surprise was made in the form of a leaked audio tape from the set of *Access Hollywood*. Trump made crude comments about women on that tape.[12] This was a forty-eight-hour blip of a scandal, and Trump proceeded to win the election a month later.

In the positive world, having an affair or being part of any sex scandal could be a career or campaign killer, even well past the era of the sexual revolution. In the neutral world, it would be damaging but probably survivable. In the negative world, violations of traditional Christian moral norms are no big deal unless they also involve transgressions of one of the ideological taboos of the new public moral order, such as a feminist stance toward gender relations. Trump's support by the religious right may have offended his opponents more than his affairs and actual sexual sins did.

The election of Donald Trump as president illustrates the radical nature of the shift to the negative world, and the ways in which the consequences of this shift aren't always obvious and extend far beyond the world of the church. Yes, the shift to the negative world has affected the standing of the church and Christians in society, but it affects the world outside the church as well.

Previously, Christian moral norms provided ethical standards for behavior in society even by non-Christians. The decline of the status of Christianity and its moral systems, cheered on by those who wished to promote, for example, greater sexual freedoms, have removed social bulwarks against the emergence of leaders with characters like Trump's. Having rejected the moral frameworks that previously governed society, those who are horrified by Trump's behaviors no longer have standards by which they can make critiques of him that will be socially viewed as objective, valid, and rooted in eternal truth. Even Trump-supporting evangelicals implicitly understand that those traditional Christian standards of public morality for leaders no longer apply in today's world.

DATING THE THREE WORLDS

The dating of these transitions is necessarily impressionistic. The transition from the positive to the neutral world was somewhat subtle and imprecise. The collapse of the Soviet empire and the end of the Cold War was clearly a major transition point. The start of the neutral world could plausibly be dated to the fall of the Berlin Wall in 1989. But I selected 1994 for the latter for two reasons.

First, that year represented the high-water mark of early '90s populism with the Republican takeover of the US House of Representatives and arguably the peak of evangelical influence within US political conservatism. This makes it a useful date for examining evangelicalism specifically.

Second, it was the year Rudolph Giuliani became mayor of New York City, signaling the urban resurgence that would have a major impact on evangelicalism. Its start predated Giuliani, but it was turbocharged by him and by the collapse in violent crime rates in big cities during the mid-1990s. This resurgence was both a product and accelerator of a trend that economist Robert Reich had in 1991 called "the secession of the successful," in which the upper middle class and the wealthy segregated themselves both geographically and culturally from the rest of society.[13]

The transition from the neutral to the negative world is more clearly evident, even to the man on the street. Something significant changed in American society during President Obama's second term, even if people can't always articulate what it was. One of the best examples of this shift is the so-called Great Awokening,[14] a term progressive technocrat Matthew Yglesias established in an article for Vox in 2019 and a change he said started in 2014[15] but which may have been triggered by the death of Trayvon Martin in 2012.

Other writers have made similar arguments about that time period. One academic study by David Rozado and his coauthors noted, "Our results show that the frequency of words that denote specific prejudice types related to ethnicity, gender, sexual, and religious orientation has markedly increased within the 2010–2019 decade across most news media outlets. This phenomenon starts prior to, but appears to accelerate after, 2015."[16] The authors point out that this started prior to Trump's election run in the 2016 cycle, so it can't be pinned entirely on his cultural influence.

Zach Goldberg at the Manhattan Institute used data from LexisNexis to examine the frequency of various terms related to wokeness in the news media and especially the *New York Times*. He found that the frequency of terms such as *social justice*, *systemic racism*, and *white privilege* being used skyrocketed from relatively low levels starting after 2012. His graphs of this became a viral sensation on the internet.[17] Clearly, something fundamentally changed in the discourse on race circa 2014, which has had a major influence on the key institutions of society.

Additionally, a major change in views toward homosexuality began in this period. The Supreme Court's *Obergefell* decision that legalized same-sex marriage across all states was handed down in 2015. This inaugurated a new legal regime in America around gender and sexuality issues that is still being elaborated. While the *Obergefell* decision itself was perhaps as much effect as cause, there was clearly a major and extremely rapid shift in public sentiment during this time period, albeit perhaps not as stark as with the Great Awokening.

In 2008, a majority of voters in California—yes, California—approved Proposition 8, a state constitutional amendment to effectively ban same-sex marriage.[18] Also in 2008, Barack Obama campaigned for president as an opponent of same-sex marriage, specifically citing his Christian faith as a rationale. He was lying about this and had already been on record as supporting same-sex marriage in the 1990s while a member of the Illinois legislature.[19] But it's notable that he felt compelled to lie about this issue and even stress Christian bona fides in order to be elected. (Hillary Clinton also publicly opposed same-sex marriage at that time.)[20] Yet by 2016, Donald Trump was personally holding up pride flags at rallies while running for president as a Republican.[21] Today, the effort to prevent people who are transgendered male-to-female from competing in girls' sports seems like a desperate rearguard action. All of this points to an incredible sea change in public morality over a short period of time.

Other indications of a major cultural shift in the early-to-mid 2010s are also evident. The mere fact that someone like Donald Trump could get elected president in 2016 was a shocking development. Social psychologist Jonathan Haidt noted that he started seeing a change in student attitudes on campus around 2013.[22] In the Christian world, evangelical pastor Rick Warren prayed at Obama's 2009 inauguration.[23] Yet by 2013, Louie Giglio was forced to withdraw from praying at Obama's second inauguration because of a controversy over his views on homosexuality.[24]

While a case could be made for any date between 2012 and 2015 marking the transition to the negative world, I selected 2014.

A FRAMEWORK IS A TOOL

As I said in the introduction, my professional background is in management consulting. This three worlds framework is similar to many other frameworks used in the consulting realm, such as the famous Boston Consulting Group matrix or the Gartner Group "magic quadrant" diagram. Like all frameworks of this type, the three worlds model is a simplification of complex phenomena designed primarily for practical purposes.

These frameworks aren't like theological or scientific models, which are claims to objective truth. They're more akin to tools. In fact, there may be many different such frameworks that can explain the same phenomenon, each useful to some people but not to others or for illuminating a different dimension of the situation. People should try out different frameworks or lenses on a problem to examine it from multiple angles in order to give them the best overall understanding of the world. Rod Dreher's Benedict Option is a related but different lens, for example, on the changes that happened with the transition to the negative world.[25]

Even if the three worlds framework doesn't explain every nuance or detail of our world, it can still be a useful tool in helping us sort through where we are and where to go from here. As a comparison, think about the way people regularly divide history into the three periods of ancient, medieval, and modern. This vastly oversimplifies a complex story, yet we continue returning to it precisely because it's so useful in thinking about the past. When we need to account for a particular nuance or trend not well accounted for in that model, we zoom in closer or change models.

Similarly, the three worlds model shows us something important about what's happened in American society over the last fifty to sixty years, but it's not all-explanatory or the last word on every matter. As we journey further into the negative world, I expect many others to develop new and different ways to think about the world we inhabit that supplement models like the three worlds or Benedict Option.

Also, the three worlds framework is designed specifically for the period *after* the midcentury consensus began to disintegrate, even if it would be valid at some level to extend the positive world further back in time. The very word *Christendom* refers to an expansive geography and lengthy history in which society was in some sense "positive" toward Christianity, even if many people did suffer harm or loss of status for their faith at times. This would include that 1950s era. However, these historic periods are highly varied, and different tools are needed to really make sense of them.

What I've labeled the positive world wasn't a world in which all was going well for Christianity. It was in fact the opposite. The positive world is defined as the period of Christian decline starting in the 1960s, during which the status of Christianity in society had fallen but not yet eroded to the point of neutrality or negativity. Many people saw alarming signs about trends in the church or society even early on in this positive world period.

When British missionary Lesslie Newbigin returned to the UK after spending most of the previous forty years in India, he discovered a culture there that in his view needed to be evangelized anew.[26] During the 1970s there was significant consternation about declining attendance in mainline denominations, as well as a significant amount of research undertaken to try to understand and respond to this. As I show in the next chapter, many of the key trends in the evangelical church were responses to this decline (as well as to other social forces).

CAUSES OF THE NEGATIVE WORLD

What caused the decline that led to Christianity descending from positive to neutral to negative status in society? This is a complex question to which no easy or certain answer can be given, but there are several directions we can explore. For example, the three worlds framework covers a period in which many have talked about the secularization of culture. The three different worlds could be seen in part as emerging from this secularization process. Secularization is a subject one could devote an entire career to studying.

Canadian philosopher Charles Taylor wrote his nine-hundred-page opus *A Secular Age* to tell a five-hundred-year-long story of secularization in the West.[27] British academic Callum Brown explained a sudden collapse of Christianity in England during the 1960s by arguing it resulted from women ceasing to view being a Christian as an essential part of their identity as women.[28]

Attempting to explain secularization or Christianity's decline is far beyond the scope of this book. But at least six major post-1964 events clearly had an impact in facilitating or even accelerating the decline of the status of Christianity in America and particularly facilitating the emergence of the negative world.

1. **THE COLLAPSE OF THE WASP ESTABLISHMENT.** As I previously noted, up through the 1950s America was largely run by a hegemonic upper class WASP establishment. While the nature of the American upper class shifted radically over the course of the nation's history, there was also remarkable continuity in important ways. For example, Kingman Brewster, president of Yale

University during the tumult of the Vietnam War era, was an eleventh generation descendent of Elder William Brewster of the *Mayflower*.[29] Members of the Adams family remained prominent in American cultural circles well into the mid-twentieth-century era. These ancient lineages, by American standards, retained prominent and powerful positions. Not for nothing was there a "Protestant" in the acronym WASP. Protestantism was a key part of their identity and an exclusionary boundary as well. Theirs was a liberal Protestantism, and many of the WASPs weren't especially religious people. But it seems unlikely that, in their day, they would ever have allowed an anti-Christian or certainly anti-Protestant attitude to dominate the country culturally as that would have eliminated part of the boundary that defined their community.

2. **THE SIXTIES SOCIAL REVOLUTION.** The late 1960s saw a major social upheaval with young adults rejecting the authority of their parents and other traditional authority figures, embracing drugs and the counterculture, protesting against the Vietnam War, rejecting aspects of the industrial economy and creating an environmental movement, experimenting with new forms of communities, and more. This was an epochal social rupture on an international scale, associated in Europe particularly with the student uprisings of 1968.

3. **THE SEXUAL REVOLUTION.** Related to the '60s social revolution, the sexual revolution of the late 1960s and '70s called into question many beliefs and practices regarding sex and family inherited as part of the Christian tradition and normalized many new practices that previously would have been forbidden. These traditional beliefs included bans against contraception,

premarital sex, pornography, homosexual practices, revised gender roles, and divorce. The full flowering of the rejection of many of the beliefs and practices didn't happen until recently, and in some cases, it's still not complete. But the changes of this era profoundly reshaped the moral DNA of the country on matters of sex and gender.

4. **THE END OF THE COLD WAR.** Undoubtedly, the collapse of the Soviet empire and the resulting end of the Cold War was a seminal event in facilitating the public rejection of Christianity by American elite culture and institutions. Because communism was an avowedly atheist system—"godless communism," as some called it—Christianity and Christian identity became part of America's fight against the Soviet bloc. For example, the phrase *under God* was added to the Pledge of Allegiance[30] and *in God We Trust* to money in the 1950s.[31] Christianity was an integral part of the regime of freedom in the West and our moral propaganda against the Soviets. Turning negative or even neutral on Christianity while the Cold War was still ongoing wasn't feasible.

5. **DEREGULATION AND CORPORATE CONSOLIDATION.** Starting in the 1970s, America began deregulating the corporate sector and especially rolling back limits on corporate concentration. As a result, a much smaller group of large companies are now much more dominant in many sectors than previously, including the banking, airline, technology, and media industries. Not every industry is dominated by an oligopoly—many small banks and credit unions still operate, for example—but there's far more concentration in many sectors, and some are de facto monopolies or oligopolies. These companies

have vast lobbying power and are more tightly connected to the state, resulting in trends like declining corporate prosecutions and access to bailouts and other government support in times of crisis. At the same time, these firms are more compliant with state and elite cultural mandates. The net result is that the market no longer acts as a meaningful check on the behavior of these firms, and they can afford to alienate half the country—as long as it's the right half of the country—and not lose business because people have fewer real alternatives. In the negative world, it can even be dangerous for a business to go against elite cultural positions.

6. **DIGITIZATION.** The move to digitization, combined with the lack of a proper regulatory framework for it, enables vast top-down control over the country. For example, even into the 1990s and later, people still conducted most financial transactions with cash or checks. Today, the majority of transactions are non-cash, such as with credit and debit cards, which means Visa and Mastercard have de facto power to determine who can engage in commerce in the US.[32] The bulk of internet traffic today is on mobile devices, and two companies control the entire market for smartphone operating system software, Apple and Google. They have significant power over deciding whether or not various kinds of companies can engage in business in the US. Unlike analogue-era essential services, such as for electricity or telephone utilities, these businesses retain discretion on with whom they will do business and with whom they will not do business. They're not treated as common carriers, and this enables vast top-down control over economic life, which by extension gives these firms vast cultural power as well.

Other key trends could be highlighted, too, such as the decline in intermediary institutions and social capital, rising income inequality, and demographic change resulting from the 1965 Immigration Act. These factors removed bulwarks that had previously supported Christianity (the WASP establishment, the Cold War) or facilitated imposition of cultural change through the development of a two-tier, top-down society with power concentrated at the top (corporate concentration, digitization).

Whatever the factors that ultimately brought about Christianity's decline in America, we find ourselves firmly planted in this new and unprecedented negative world, where for the first time in the four-hundred-year history of America, the culture as a whole and key institutions of society have turned negative toward Christianity and Christian morality. Before looking at how we should respond to and live in this negative world, let's first consider how evangelicals responded to the positive and neutral worlds that preceded the negative world.

CHAPTER 2

STRATEGIES FOR THE POSITIVE AND NEUTRAL WORLDS

MAINLINE DENOMINATIONS LIKE THE EPISCOPALIANS, Presbyterians, Lutherans, and similarly traditional groups dominated the Protestant landscape up to the 1950s. The alternatives to the mainline were generally considered lower-status, such as fundamentalist churches. Starting in the 1940s, people like Billy Graham and Carl F. H. Henry helped crystalize the neo-evangelical movement, which attempted to navigate between those two poles. This emerging evangelicalism would hold firm to traditional Christian beliefs but be more culturally and socially relevant and less sectarian.

As the mainline denominations slipped into a major decline in the 1970s, evangelicalism proved to be more adaptable to changing times and grew into a mainstream cultural phenomenon. In contrast to both the mainline and fundamentalist churches, this characteristic of cultural adaptability to maintain relevance has been a hallmark of the evangelical movement over the past fifty years. It was so successful in this that fundamentalism (as a distinct, separate movement) has now been absorbed into most people's conception of evangelicalism today.

Evangelicalism, then, became a major force in America during this initial period of declining Christian cultural influence. The ability to successful adapt to a state of decline is, in many ways, built into evangelicalism and might be considered its greatest strength. At the very least, it gives many a reason to be optimistic that evangelicals will adapt once again, this time to the negative world. But how did different groups of evangelicals adapt to the positive and neutral worlds?

Grouping or classifying the various streams within evangelicalism can be done in many different ways. In his 2020 book *Reformed Resurgence*, sociologist Brad Vermurlen identified four different groups: New Calvinist, Neo-Anabaptist, Emergent, and "Mainstream" Evangelicalism.[1] In his book *To Change the World*, sociologist James Davison Hunter, whose analysis wasn't limited to evangelicals, divided the Christian world into Right, Left, and Neo-Anabaptist.[2] As I previously noted, the most common model for categorizing Protestants in social science surveys[3] divides Protestants into the three categories of Mainline, Evangelical, and Black Protestant.

Just as my three worlds framework for categorizing recent American history is a utilitarian model, these classification systems are likewise models chosen because they were useful for certain applications. Grouping churches and people within the evangelical world can also be done in many different ways. My interest is in how evangelicals adapted to the changing landscape of the three worlds, so I group them according to broad strategic approaches. Three models in particular stand out. In the positive world, these were the *culture war* strategy and the *seeker sensitivity* strategy. In the neutral world, the strategy was *cultural engagement*.

Unlike with the names of the three worlds, which are specific to my framework, these are all terms already in use within the evangelical world, sometimes meaning different things to different people. My framework uses them to describe broad families of people, churches, and organizations that, while in many cases not formally organized or aligned, shared various commonalities in how they responded to the changing cultural landscape of post-1960s America. As with the three worlds, this model is my own framework. Not all evangelical churches fit cleanly into these categories, but they do represent three general trends running through the evangelical church landscape.

Again, others have divided the evangelical world into different groupings. But from the standpoint of looking at the interaction of evangelicalism with the changing societal view of Christianity through the positive, neutral, and negative worlds, these three groups are particularly useful to examine, and I describe each of them in turn.

THE CULTURE WARRIORS

The *culture war* strategy is often called the Religious Right and is the best-known movement of the positive world era. We must remember that while the positive world was one in which society still viewed Christianity and its moral systems positively, this was still an era of decline for Christianity. It was also an era of navigating significant cultural change, the fruit of the '60s social revolutions and the sexual revolution that extended into the 1970s.

The social changes of this time were alarming to many Christians as well as to others of a more traditionally minded nature who believed their moral values were under assault by secular radicals. They sensed the declining influence of

Christian morality, and their response was to fight back in order to arrest or reverse this decline and take back the culture. This led to the emergence of the culture war movement, part of a larger New Right movement of the 1970s and '80s.[4] The very name of the leading culture war organization, Moral Majority, speaks to a world in which it was at least plausible to claim that Christians still represented the moral values of the majority of the country.

Up to and through the 1970s, evangelicals had predominantly voted for the Democratic Party. Jimmy Carter, a former Southern Baptist Sunday school teacher, was the first evangelical US president, and he won the white Baptist vote 56 to 43 percent.[5] *Newsweek* magazine proclaimed 1976, the year of his election, the "year of the evangelical."[6] As late as 1983, sociologist James Davison Hunter found that a plurality of evangelicals continued to identify as Democrats.[7] But under the influence of leaders like Jerry Falwell, this group firmly realigned into the Republican Party during the 1980s and became the Religious Right we know today. Televangelist Pat Robertson ran for president as a Republican in 1988, and evangelicals remain one of the Republican Party's most loyal voting bloc. About 80 percent of self-identified evangelicals who voted, voted for Donald Trump in 2016.[8]

In the 1970s and 1980s, Religious Right culture warriors took a highly combative stance toward the emerging secular culture, in particular fighting against abortion and other aspects of the sexual revolution. By and large leaders associated with the culture wars were far away from the citadels of culture; many of them were situated in culturally backwater locations. They tended to use their own platforms to reach people, such as with direct mail and paid-for television shows.[9] They were initially funded primarily by donations from their flocks of followers, which gave them an attention-grabbing, marketing-driven style. Groups like the Christian Coalition would later raise money from bigger donors as they became more explicitly aligned with the GOP.

Major culture war figures included Jerry Falwell Sr. of the Moral Majority (Lynchburg, Virginia), Pat Robertson of the Christian Broadcasting Network (Virginia Beach), James Dobson of Focus on the Family (Colorado Springs), Ralph Reed of the Christian Coalition, and televangelists like Jimmy Swaggart (Baton Rouge).

SEEKER SENSITIVITY

Seeker sensitivity was another strategy of the positive world movement. It was pioneered in the 1970s and '80s at suburban megachurches like Bill Hybels's Willow Creek Community Church (South Barrington, Illinois)[10] and Rick Warren's Saddleback Church (Orange County, California). The very term *seeker sensitive*[11] supposes an underlying friendliness to Christianity. It's a model that also inherently assumes large numbers of people are actively seeking association with the Christian church and Christianity.

Like the culture warriors, the leaders of the seeker sensitive movement observed the decline in church attendance and the cultural change happening around them. But rather than engage in war with the culture, their response was to reposition the church to be more relevant to changing consumer tastes in order to increase their market uptake. It was a business school approach to Christianity. A businessman's son, Bill Hybels walked door to door in suburban Chicago surveying the unchurched about why they didn't attend church.[12] Note again the positive world environment of Hybels's survey and approach. His underlying assumption was that at some level people knew they should be going to church. In a neutral world such a survey would receive many befuddled responses, while in today's negative world it might encounter outright hostility.

By designing a church that stylistically appealed to non-attenders, Hybels was able to attract large numbers of people. Seeker sensitive churches like Willow Creek downplayed or eliminated denominational affiliations, theological distinctives, and religious traditions. They adopted informal liturgies and embraced contemporary music styles. Seeker sensitivity operated in a therapeutic register, sometimes explicitly—the Christian psychologist Henry Cloud has spoken at Willow Creek many times.[13] These churches were approachable and non-threatening to non-churchgoing people in the broader culture.

The Jesus Movement of the 1960s and '70s, a Christian expression of the counterculture, paved the way for this movement, leading to what is now known as contemporary Christian music, today a fixture of seeker sensitive churches. It also helped create a more relaxed and casual approach to faith.[14] And seeker sensitivity grew in part because these churches were started in rapidly growing suburban areas. They benefited from suburbanization (and white flight), as well as the emergence of the baby boomers into mature adulthood. Seeker sensitive churches were, and to some extent still are, associated with boomers and their cultural values. While their style was different from the combativeness of culture war leaders like Falwell and Robertson, the people leading and attending these churches tended to be politically conservative, often voting Republican in line with the Religious Right.

Today, there exist many large suburban megachurches of this general type in the United States, often nondenominational, that to some extent represent the evangelical mainstream.

CULTURAL ENGAGEMENT

The neutral world emerged concurrently with the resurgence of America's urban centers from their nadir in the 1970s and '80s. The flow of college-degreed Christians into these urban centers picked up steam in the 1990s and created a different kind of evangelical social base, one shaped by urban cultural sensibilities rather than rural or suburban ones. This led to the creation of a new strategy of *cultural engagement*. The pioneers and leading lights of this strategy were frequently based in these reviving major global cities or operated in culturally similar college towns.

Conceptualizing the cultural engagement movement can also be done in many ways. One approach is to think of it as seeker sensitivity for the cities.[15] Just as seeker sensitive churches arose with the emergence of baby boomer suburbia, cultural engagement churches developed with the reemergence of major urban centers like New York City and Washington, DC. Their motifs were varied in keeping with urban diversity.

Some of these urban churches had more traditional or formal liturgies.[16] Others were "hip cool."[17] Still others targeted emerging immigrant communities or sought to be intentionally multiethnic.[18] They tended to downplay flashpoint social issues like abortion or homosexuality. Instead, they emphasized the gospel or "Jesus," often in a therapeutic register similar to seeker sensitivity, and priorities like helping the poor and select forms of social activism. They were frequently more intellectually and artistically engaged than the other evangelical groups, in line with their more educated demographics.[19]

But unlike the seeker sensitives, they couldn't assume a latent desire to attend church. They had to earn a hearing for the gospel.

A second way to think about them is as taking the opposite

approach of the culture warriors. Rather than fighting against the culture, they were explicitly positive toward it. They valued and affirmed urban lifestyles, vocation and career orientation,[20] and the life of the mind.[21] Rather than denouncing secular culture, they sought to confidently meet that culture on its own terms in a pluralistic public square. They believed that Christianity could still be articulated in a compelling way and had something to offer in that environment, even as they wanted to challenge aspects of the culture that were in conflict with Christian teaching. They wanted a presence in the forums of the secular elite media, not just engagement with Christian media or their own platforms.[22]

They also tended to be more publicly apolitical than most positive world Christians, though this broke down during 2016 when some in this group vociferously opposed Donald Trump.[23]

Most of the urban church world and many parachurch organizations embraced the cultural engagement strategy. And some suburban megachurches have shifted that direction. Major figures and groups include Tim Keller of Redeemer Presbyterian Church (New York City), Hillsong Church (New York City, Los Angeles, and other global cities), Veritas Forum (Cambridge, Massachusetts), contemporary artist Makoto Fujimura (Princeton, New Jersey, and New York City), and author Andy Crouch (Philadelphia).

THE THREE MODELS CONTRASTED WITH NIEBUHR'S FRAMEWORK

Again, these three models—culture war, seeker sensitivity, and cultural engagement—aren't intended to be the only possible categorization scheme for evangelical churches, entities, and people. Nor can every part of evangelicalism be easily fit into these three groups. While many people within these groups do maintain formal and informal relationships with one another, these groups are intended to represent three families of strategic responses to changing culture rather than integrated organizations or structured alliances. Additionally, while some of these approaches were intentionally strategic in character,[24] these models also developed and evolved organically as well.

Because the purpose of my framework is to examine how the evangelical church responded to a changing culture, it should not be directly compared with other models created for different purposes. However, it is difficult to avoid engaging with the most well-known contemporary model for understanding the way Christianity relates to culture, the five-fold model outlined by H. Richard Niebuhr in his landmark 1951 book *Christ and Culture.*[25] Though shaped by the Christianity of 1950s America, this book tries to identify several timeless models for relating Christianity and culture: Christ against culture, Christ of culture, Christ above culture, Christ and culture in paradox, and Christ transforming culture.

Niebuhr's concerns are primarily *theological*, namely, how Christians have sought to reconcile or relate reason and revelation, the natural law and Christ's law. He refers to "culture" in part because reason and natural law always come to us through cultural interpretations, never directly. Christians in Niebuhr's models act the way they do because of their theological positions about how Christ and culture are related. The strategies I've identified, by contrast, are primarily *strategic* ones based on observation, relating how the evangelical church *pragmatically* responded to American culture in particular contexts. I don't claim that these strategies were primarily informed by theology, though undoubtedly theological and other dispositions played a role in their development.

Nevertheless, Niebuhr's categories do lend themselves toward certain responses to culture. In his Christ against culture model, for example, Christ's law supplants culture, leading to a response of separation from the world as in 1 John. Examples would be Catholic monks or Anabaptist sects like the Amish. Tim Keller undertook to map these in a contemporary context in his 2012 book *Center Church*.[26] Keller sees Niebuhr's "Christ transforming culture" informing "transformationalist" approaches, including those derived from the neo-Calvinism of Dutch theologian and politician Abraham Kuyper, as well as the religious right.[27] This would probably include the culture war approach from my model.[28] Keller sees Niebuhr's "Christ of culture" and "Christ above culture" models informing "relevance" approaches. In these he includes many megachurches, the emerging church, and the mainline churches.

I would describe seeker sensitivity[29] as a relevance approach, and I would also describe cultural engagement as a relevance approach, though sometimes with transformationalist aspirations.[30] Keller's "counterculturalist" model appears to come from Niebuhr's "Christ against culture," and his "two kingdoms" model from Niebuhr's "Christ and culture in paradox." These contain predominantly smaller groups like the neo-Anabaptists that don't map cleanly to my three models.[31] In summary, while my three models weren't derived from Niebuhr's framework, they can be situated relative to it.

DIFFERENT PEOPLE, NOT JUST DIFFERENT STRATEGIES

Culture war, seeker sensitivity, and cultural engagement represented differentiated responses to the positive and neutral worlds. But they also reflected other theological, sociological, and cultural differences among the various groups. With the key figures I previously identified, one could, for example, see a roughly geographic split, with culture warriors representing rural and backwater areas, seeker sensitives representing suburbia, and cultural engagers representing the city.[32]

This relates to class differences as well. The culture warriors were mostly middle- and lower-middle class. Their leaders may have had college degrees, but their followers frequently did not.[33] The seeker sensitives and cultural engagers were more solidly middle class (or higher in some cases) and typically better educated.[34] Cultural engagement was a higher-status movement than seeker sensitivity, because in America, the city, with which this movement is associated, is higher status than the suburbs.

Dispositionally, the culture warriors had a fundamentalist sensibility and often came from that tradition. Jerry Falwell had a fundamentalist background, for example.[35] The seeker sensitives and cultural engagers had a more neo-evangelical sensibility.[36] Fundamentalism prioritized doctrinal purity and was frequently separatist and hostile to outsiders or to those who would compromise on biblical fidelity. The neo-evangelicalism of the 1940s was an attempt to create a fundamentalism that would reach the mainstream. Its priorities have been more missional than doctrinal. Seen primarily as sensibilities, this split between doctrinal or confessional purity and missional focus or revivalism has persistently manifested itself in different ways throughout American religious history.[37]

There were also other differences. The culture warriors attracted large numbers of Pentecostal charismatics such as Pat Robertson (though there was some tension between them and the non-charismatic portions of that movement).[38] The seeker sensitives and cultural engagers are much less Pentecostal.

Those who do affirm the continuation of the charismatic gifts of the Holy Spirit are low key about it. The culture warriors were also heavily shaped by the Cold War—they weren't just culture warriors but cold warriors. The very name of Falwell's Liberty University attests to this association with America's fight against communism.[39] This was often linked to a fervor about the end times, which many culture warriors saw as imminent. The cultural engagers, by contrast, were better adapted to a post–Cold War era and reflected an end of history[40] perspective rather than an end times perspective. They were no longer burdened by Cold War considerations.

What we see is that these three models were responses to the cultural changes of the positive and neutral worlds, but the specifics of how these approaches were developed were also in part a product of the geographic, cultural, and theological backgrounds of their creators.

THE DAWN OF THE NEGATIVE WORLD

The deterioration of the standing of Christianity in the 1970s led to the development of the culture war and seeker sensitivity strategies in the positive world. The transition to the neutral world led to the emergence of the cultural engagement strategy. And the primary strategy advocated for the negative world is Rod Dreher's Benedict Option, outlined in his book of the same name.[41]

Dreher is not an evangelical; he's Eastern Orthodox, and he openly admits his limited understanding of the evangelical world. His book is titled after a Catholic monk and prominently features a monastery. Dreher may have underestimated Protestant suspicion of monastic imagery, because naming his strategy after the founder of Catholic monasticism undoubtedly contributed to its poor reception in the evangelical world. While his intent in drawing on the model of the monastery was to focus on their stable, strong communities and how creating those today is critical for the future of the church, many saw the Benedict Option as a strategy of withdrawal from the world. This also led many evangelicals, to whom the Great Commission is central, to view it skeptically.

But even when you take these factors into account, evangelicals appeared to have been excessively negative toward the book. For example, *Christianity Today*, the flagship evangelical magazine, commissioned four people to write about *The Benedict Option*, all of whom had significant criticisms of it.[42] We also see this rejection of Dreher's proposal in that we have not yet developed a more evangelical-friendly version of or alternative to it. No major evangelical strategic approaches for the negative world have emerged. American evangelicals are largely operating as though they're still living in the lost positive and neutral worlds. The rejection of Dreher's Benedict Option, I argue, wasn't about too much Catholic terminology or disagreements on its strategic elements. It was rooted in a lack of recognition that cultural conditions have fundamentally changed for Christianity. Evangelicals had not—and to a great extent still have not—recognized that we now live in the negative world.

HOW THE NEGATIVE WORLD CHANGED THE MODELS

Although evangelicals have not yet developed a ministry strategy specifically for the negative world, the transition to this world has had major consequences for evangelicalism. The pressures of the negative world are more intense in higher status and more elite domains, where secular ideologies most in conflict with Christianity are also most embedded. Because different evangelicals have differing degrees of exposure to this pressure, the shift to the negative world has put different types and levels of pressure on the different evangelical groups.

However, transition to the negative world is affecting each of the models I identified. As with politics, these pressures intersect with different social groups and strategic positionings, producing change, conflict, and realignment within the evangelical world, particularly affecting the cultural engagement and culture war models.

CULTURAL ENGAGEMENT AND THE NEGATIVE WORLD

Of these groups, the cultural engagers are clearly most at risk from the transition to the negative world. Although the shift from the positive to the neutral world represented a downward turn in Christianity's standing within society, the cultural engagement strategy characteristic of the neutral world was actually higher status than the culture war strategy. For example, contemporary artist Makoto Fujimura has been respected in the art world at large for the quality of his work, with his Christianity openly recognized as an artistic influence. He's received positive reviews in the *Los Angeles Times*[43] and a positive profile in the *New York Times*,[44] and he's painted live on stage at Carnegie Hall.[45]

Cultural engagement leaders have been treated as respectable by elite secular society in ways the culture warriors never were. They have a cultural status to lose that the lower-status culture war Christians of the positive world never had to begin with.

An example of how the negative world threatens this loss of social status is what happened to Tim Keller at Princeton

Seminary in 2017. Keller was slated to receive the seminary's Abraham Kuyper Award and give an associated lecture. It's hard to think of anyone more thoughtful and well-spoken than Keller, but students still protested his award because he holds to gender theology that restricts ordained ministry to men and affirms men as the head of the home. The award was retracted although Keller was still allowed to give a talk.[46] If even Tim Keller is too evangelical in his beliefs for a moderate mainline seminary, it's hard to see how other evangelicals could get a hearing there.

Cultural engagers are also much more likely to live in urban environments, work in high-paying and prestigious professions, and enjoy the social milieu of the upper middle class (historic architecture, pour-over coffees, farm-to-table restaurants, artisanal goods, luxury gyms, and the like). The environments in which they live and work are majority secular progressive where the negative world culture of secular progressivism is most intense. These are cultural environments where individuals are being canceled—no longer supported, or even fired—because of beliefs and statements that deviate from the acceptable progressive ideology of the negative world. Those who come from a seeker sensitivity or suburban megachurch environment will feel similar pressures if they're living and working in more upscale, corporate suburbs.

Those who live in the upper-middle-class or elite world are exposed to much greater negative world pressure than those who live and work in environments that still retain elements of the positive or neutral world. They face more risk and a greater social cost when they run afoul of the current secular progressive line. This risk and pressure they're under is often under-appreciated by more middle-class or blue-collar Christians living in environments like small towns, rural communities, or remnants of the Bible Belt that are still in some ways positive toward Christianity.

To adapt, some of those who live and work in these hostile environments have been turning away from engagement in favor of an evolving synchronization with secular elite culture—particularly on matters such as race, immigration, and the MeToo movement—aligning more closely with progressive cultural and political positions.

At the same time, they've further softened their stance and rhetoric on other traditionally evangelical flashpoint social issues. For example, they increasingly talk about being holistically pro-life,[47] emphasizing aid to single mothers or support of immigration as pro-life positions rather than just opposition to abortion. While holding to traditional teachings on sexuality, they tend to speak less about Christianity's moral prohibitions[48] and talk more about how the church should be a welcoming place for "sexual minorities" as well as emphasizing the ways the church has failed to treat them well.[49] This approach has been particularly attractive to upper-middle-class, urban, and highly educated evangelicals.

In short, the cultural engagement strategy, as one of relevance, sometimes with transformational emphases, has had to shift to try to remain relevant. It has also come to see secular movements such as the present emphasis on racial justice as vehicles for cultural transformation. The net result has been a more syncretistic approach.

CULTURE WARRIORS AND THE NEGATIVE WORLD

For their part, the culture warriors and the Religious Right, who persisted through the neutral world, have evolved toward Trumpist populism in the negative world. They are Trumpist not just because they support Donald Trump politically, but also in that they've embraced his key positions on issues like immigration and trade restrictions—and sometimes post-liberal politics as well. They are populist in that they tend to attack elites, including evangelical elites, in the name of the masses.

They have also jettisoned some historic Religious Right touchstones, such as a concern for personal morality and character in political leaders in favor of a more realpolitik approach as shown in their embrace of Trump. This is a clear example of deformation and opens them to the charge of hypocrisy. Having denounced Bill Clinton as disqualified for office because of low moral character, with Trump they argued that other factors could trump, as it were, character.

It may well be that some of this group felt like no national leaders spoke for them or their concerns, leaving Trump as their only option. Nevertheless, this represents a clear change from the past. And some have gone beyond this, participating in a sort of personality cult around Trump or describing him in messianic terms. Former Texas governor Rick Perry, for example, referred to Trump as God's "chosen one."[50] Traditional social issues like abortion do remain very important to them. They also continue to be lower in economic status and education levels and tend to live away from the nation's cultural centers.

The culture war, as a transformationalist strategy, has been forced to confront a culture not amenable to being transformed through politics, even should conservatives win elections. This has led to an openness to more radical leaders and ideas and a more Machiavellian approach to politics.

EVANGELICAL CONFLICT
AND REALIGNMENT

These shifts have produced conflict and realignment within the evangelical world for multiple reasons. The first was Donald Trump and his embrace by the culture warriors. Their support of a man of such low and boorish character horrified some people of a generally conservative disposition who might otherwise have remained part of the Religious Right. These are the people for whom personal character and class still mattered. Some historically center-right, middle-class suburbanites, for example, were very turned off by Trump. Others were appalled by the presence of the theologically aberrant figures among Trump's religious inner circle, such as prosperity preacher Paula White.[51]

Similarly, but in the opposite direction, some of this same group of generally center-right mainstream evangelicals became alarmed by what appears to be an in-progress abandonment of traditional beliefs on sexuality and the embrace of hard-left secular positions on race, such as payment of racial reparations to blacks,[52] by some cultural engagement leaders. Trump and wokeness are the two key polarizers re-sorting evangelicals.

This split has been acrimonious at times. The culture warriors have been fiercely hostile toward "the establishment." Hostility to elites is part of the populist effect, and their combativeness toward what they perceive as theological drift flows from their fundamentalist sensibility. For their part, the cultural engagers in upper-middle-class milieux have also adopted a separatist approach.[53] They're keen to show the world they're not at all aligned with the Trumpist culture warriors, and in some cases they've harshly denounced them. In effect, they've declared their own culture war, but theirs is against other evangelicals rather than against the world.[54]

These divisions are ripping churches and other evangelical institutions apart.[55] One reason is that they aren't perfectly divided among the various groups. Some fundamentalist churches may be purely culture war. Some progressive-leaning urban churches may be almost entirely aligned with cultural engagers. But other churches are a mix. In particular, the mainstream of suburban megachurches deriving from the seeker sensitivity movement tend to have a mix of different people, including many in the middle who could be pulled in either direction depending on whether they're more allergic to Trump or to secular left racial politics.

Even within the various tribes there are dissenters. Prominent conservative columnist David French[56] might have once aligned with the culture war camp, but his negative reaction to Trump and preexisting personal and professional relationships in the neoconservative world turned him into a fierce opponent of the Trumpists.[57] Similarly, some evangelicals in elite urban centers aren't happy with hard-left secular race politics in their church. Some new churches are explicitly advertising that they are "non-woke" to cater to them.[58]

Evangelicalism now finds itself in a state of flux, and its future as a coherent movement is in doubt. In part, this results from its failure to develop strategies designed for the negative world in which Christians are now a moral *minority* and secular society is actively negative toward the faith. The previous strategies aren't adequate to today's realities and are shifting in sometimes unhealthy ways under the pressures of the negative world.

LOOKING FORWARD

Obviously, it's impossible to predict the future. But the past suggests that the culture warriors can survive, if only in a diminished form. Those with a fundamentalist sensibility did survive with their faith and churches intact when the major Protestant denominations adopted liberal theologies. But it would mean a return to a geographically and demographically limited backwoods Christianity devoid of public or cultural influence.

The future of the cultural engagers and megachurch people who have turned toward cultural synchronization, however, looks grimmer. The much-discussed failures of the evangelical elite[59] can't be understood without reference to the way the ground rapidly and fundamentally shifted under them with the transition to the negative world. Their desire to remain relevant in secular elite society, their social gospel–type transformational focus, and the embrace of current secular academic theories are reminiscent of what happened to the mainline denominations (though this time the secular theories are from the social rather than natural sciences).

Those denominations, once well attended and socially prestigious, have lost a large share of their members over the course of the last fifty years, and those who remain in the pews skew elderly. The theology in some of these congregations is but a thin veneer on top of secular progressivism. The results could easily be the same for cultural engagement evangelicals: retention of cultural cachet, for a time, but ultimately the slow loss of adherents and theological orthodoxy.

But these are simply projections of present trends into the future. Again, evangelicalism has been nothing if not adaptable. What would it look like for it to successfully adapt to the negative world? That is what the remainder of this book will address.

CHAPTER 3

STRATEGIES FOR THE NEGATIVE WORLD

THE THREE WORLDS MODEL IS SPECIFIC TO THE PERIOD of Christian decline in America since 1964. But putting it in a broader perspective shows that the negative world is more than just a phase in recent American history; it represents something fundamentally new. For the first time in the four-hundred-year history of this country, society now disfavors Christianity.

This is not unique to America; it's been happening throughout the Western world formerly known as Christendom as it secularizes. French philosopher Chantal Delsol discusses this in her book *The End of the Christian World* and elsewhere.[1] She argues that rather than a forward evolution, this represents a reversion to a pre-Christian form of religion and society she calls the "return of paganism."[2] In pagan society there's a separation of religion (rites) and morality, resulting in an official "state morality," one we see in our world today in the ever more coercively enforced ideological lines of today's left. This regression toward the old pre-Christian religious model has produced what Delsol calls a "normative inversion"[3] in our moral system on matters like abortion and sexuality.

One does not have to agree with Delsol's repaganization thesis to recognize that something radical, consequential, and indeed unprecedented has been happening to the relationship of society and culture at large to Christianity in the West. We find something similar in the work of philosopher Charles Taylor, who sees secularization as the outworking of tectonic forces stretching back to before the Protestant Reformation. It should thus come to us as no surprise that the evangelical strategies developed in the positive and neutral worlds weren't able to fundamentally reverse this trend as though it were merely an intellectual, social, or political fad.

But their accomplishments should not be understated. Evangelicalism's vigor and ability to adapt in the United States has kept Christianity alive and vibrant here to a much greater extent than it is in Europe. Without that, the negative world would be a much more difficult place. We should be grateful for what the previous generations accomplished. And the limits of previous approaches should also lead to humility about any strategies developed for the negative world.

It's also the case that while the culture war, seeker sensitivity, and cultural engagement models of the previous eras are coming under pressure and are no longer as effective, each one got some things right. In adapting to the negative world, the best and most relevant parts of the other models should be honored and retained. The culture warriors, for example, understood that sometimes it's necessary to be lower status and unpopular with society's elites. The seeker sensitives were focused on the Great Commission and ensuring there were no artificial, man-made barriers between people and the gospel. The cultural engagers understood the value of the life of the mind, as well as having a more sophisticated understanding of cultural power than other evangelicals, drawing heavily from the insights of sociologist James Davison Hunter, author of *To Change the World*.

Other Protestant traditions and even, as we shall see, the Catholic Church have things to teach us too. The mainline churches shaped a powerful leadership culture for our society for decades, one whose lack today we feel keenly. And the black church shows us how to remain faithful in the face of deep injustice and unmerited suffering. There's much within American Christian history to draw on in crafting a negative world response.

THE UNKNOWN TERRITORY

Yet there are no simple answers as to how to live as people and as the church in the negative world. Like the Hebrews crossing the Jordan after forty years in the desert, evangelicals have entered unfamiliar territory. Whatever the reality of life in the desert had been for the Israelites, it was the only one they'd ever known. They knew they'd been promised the land of Canaan, but they'd never been there, and they knew it was occupied by powerful tribes that wouldn't let go of it without a fight. As they prepared to cross the Jordan, the people were told, "When you see the ark of the covenant of the LORD your God, and the Levitical priests carrying it, you are to move out from your positions and follow it. Then you will know which way to go, since you have never been this way before" (Joshua 3:3–4).

Similarly, American evangelicals have never been this way before. Whether or not we've recognized it, we've been moving into the unknown territory of the negative world. Yet we have to step forward, keeping our eyes firmly pointed toward Jesus, trusting in him with all our hearts, knowing he will make our paths straight (Proverbs 3:5–6).

Finding a path in this fundamentally unknown world will require a different approach from the strategies of the past. Consider again the business strategy approach Bill Hybels used when pioneering the seeker sensitive model to establish Willow Creek Community Church. He identified his target market, conducted research to find out why people weren't being well served by the existing churches in the area, and created a product that they were ready to buy. This approach worked well then, and it's still applicable in many situations today.

But a business strategy approach is most useful when there's a well-defined problem, a known market to address, or a space adjacent to something that's already understood. When journeying into the more fundamentally unknown, a different set of skills is required, one based on an older model of exploration.

THINKING LIKE AN EXPLORER

Dwight Gibson is the chief explorer of The Exploration Group, a consultancy that seeks to apply the methods of old explorers to challenges in today's world. Gibson observes that exploration of the genuinely unknown was once common and led to some of the legendary and consequential events in history. But in the early twentieth century, most of the places that had been either unknown or unexplored by Westerners were mapped.

At the same time, science and engineering also dramatically improved. The West turned away from and lost the mindset and skills of exploration in favor of engineering and management, professions that were just then fully coming into their own.[4] Exceptions are in areas like space exploration or extreme sports, which might account for why they fascinate many people.

This loss of the mindset and techniques of exploration and the overdominance of approaches based on management or business strategy have left us lacking some of the tools needed to successfully venture into the truly unknown. Only in select places such as the startup world has something of the exploration mindset survived. Technology investor Peter Thiel's book on startups is called *From Zero to One*. The title refers to the fact that creating the first version of something entirely new out of nothing is fundamentally different from replicating that one new thing into many. One is exploration. The other management.

Gibson uses a methodology called ExPLORE to describe the exploration method he derived from studying historic explorers. This is an acrostic that refers to developing *Expectations*, acting decisively when coming to *X-roads* (crossroads), and *Pondering* deeply, taking note of *Landmarks* in order to *Orienteer* through new territory. Then explorers can celebrate new *Realizations* and *Evaluate* next steps.

Today, evangelicals, evangelical churches, and evangelical institutions are standing at Gibson's crossroads. There's a decision to make. Do we act decisively to move forward with exploring this new negative world territory? Or do we turn back to business as usual, denial, or hoping God calls us home before the negative world's new pressures hit us personally? Will we imitate Joshua, who boldly led the Hebrew people across the Jordan into the unexplored promised land? Or will we imitate Hezekiah, who when faced with a prophecy of doom for his people and even his children after he died, said, "'The word of the LORD you have spoken is good'" . . . For he thought, 'Will there not be peace and security in my lifetime?'" (2 Kings 20:19)?

The choice to move forward from the crossroads doesn't mean fully or even mostly understanding the new landscape before being confronted with difficult choices. And even once oriented to the landscape, it will surely continue changing. Things are going to happen regardless of preparation, and decisions will have to be made. That's part of what it means to explore. But like the Hebrews, we can be confident that despite all the uncertainty and risk, the God who has promised never to fail us or forsake us will carry us successfully to our ultimate destination in his kingdom.

Unlike in the positive and neutral worlds, in the negative world one or two general strategies will not be sufficient. Today's America is in many ways simply much more complex and too diverse for a one-size-fits-all model. There's more racial diversity, obviously. That's one important dimension of a more complex landscape. But Christians also live in a variety of different personal circumstances. The strategies that will work for people living and working in Manhattan will be different from the strategies that will work for people living and working in suburban Dallas—or in rural West Virginia, or in a Mexican immigrant neighborhood in Chicago, or in any number of places in America. Someone with a culture war inclination will do things differently from someone with a cultural engagement sensibility, even if they both successfully adapt to the negative world.

Creating models for the evangelical church in the negative world will thus involve a large number of people exploring various parts of the landscape. It will involve a lot of trial and error. It will involve experimentation. It will involve false starts and the ability to adapt and adjust quickly. It will require wide but loose alliances and networks with a lot of information sharing.

LIVING AS A MORAL MINORITY

While much about the negative world is unknown, some is known. The paradigmatic positive world's culture war organization was Moral Majority. Its very name speaks to a time when it was possible to claim that Christians represented a majority of the country. That may have been wrong even at the time, but like Richard Nixon's Silent Majority, it was at least a plausible claim. Today, that's simply not true. Christians are now, as it were, a moral minority, even if a sizable one.[5] This means changing to act like one.

Because since the 1980s evangelicals have been closely aligned with political conservatism and the Republican Party,[6] it's easy to conflate the prospects of evangelicalism with the prospects for Republican electoral victory. The Republican Party is in a period of turmoil, but it clearly has a large following. It's easy to imagine scenarios in which Republicans control the presidency, Congress, and most state houses. In fact, many states are already overwhelmingly Republican controlled. But Republicans winning electoral majorities doesn't mean evangelical Christians are a majority, or that the Republican Party will advance evangelical religious priorities, or that Republicans will even in many cases defend evangelical church teachings against a skeptical culture. I explore this more in both chapter 5 and chapter 12.

The voting base of the Republican Party is increasingly made up of non-Christians or post-Christians. One example where this is evident is in the youth cohorts, where young Gen Z men who vote Republican are often followers of the largely non-Christian "dissident right" groups[7] or fall into hedonistic demographics like "barstool conservatives."[8] The Republican Party of the future likely represents a growing post-Christian right for America.

Evangelicals, even when combined with other Christian groups like Roman Catholics, are now a minority in the United States, at least when it comes to those who adhere to traditional Christian beliefs. This was illustrated by the results of the 2022 midterm elections held after the reversal of *Roe v. Wade*. The results of every one of the abortion-related ballot initiatives came down in favor of abortion. Even in Kentucky, a very conservative state, voters rejected a constitutional amendment that would merely have confirmed that the state constitution does not contain a right to abortion.[9] This suggests that a majority of Americans want abortion to be legal at some level. Similarly, Congress codified same-sex marriage into federal law around the same time—with significant Republican support.

While not conclusive, these events suggest that traditional evangelical ethical positions—or at least support for them—are now in the minority, even if they remain supported by a large and important segment of the Republican voting base. Making the difficult but necessary adjustments to think of the evangelical church in this way is just one aspect of adapting to the negative world.

The negative world thus augurs for a shift in emphasis away from relevance and transformation toward being a counterculture. Unlike with Niebuhr in his pure form, I don't argue for this from a theological position but a contextual one. A society that's supermajority Protestant and Christian normative, as the United States once was, is very different from today's society, which is demographically pluralistic and negative toward Christianity. In his analysis of Niebuhr, Tim Keller describes these types of shifts as cultural "seasonality," arguing that the West has shifted from summer to autumn in terms of the relationship of society and Christianity.[10] The strategies of the previous worlds are no longer as relevant to the negative world.

Because in most cases evangelical ministry approaches aren't excessively tied to particular theological positions, we aren't limited to drawing from just one model. The themes I lay out for the negative world will strengthen the emphasis on being a counterculture, but that doesn't mean an Amish-like withdrawal. We should continue to be as relevant as possible to carry out the Great Commission and pursue transformation where there's an opportunity to do so. But as we will see, in order to do those things, we'll need to be more intentional with regard to our own individual, family, and community lives.

THE ROAD FORWARD

In 2009, I won an international innovation competition for ideas to boost public transit ridership in Chicago. My winning entry was a 50-point plan that covered every major aspect of this task.[11] My proposal used a traditional business strategy approach of the type I employed when working as a management consultant.

Yet as we consider how evangelical Christians should navigate the unexplored negative world, I have no similar business strategy or 50-point master plan to share with you. Instead, I've identified a set of three starter ideas across each of the three key domains of our evangelical life: personal, institutional, and missional.

- **PERSONAL**—how we live and structure our individual lives and that of our households
- **INSTITUTIONAL**—how we do the same for our churches, as well as for other evangelical institutions like parachurch ministries, Christian colleges, and Christian-owned businesses
- **MISSIONAL**—how we find ways to carry out the Great Commission with evangelization and by loving our neighbors

Some of my suggestions are more direct than others. Each of them require evangelicals and their leaders to figure out exactly how to apply them in their own unique situations and cultural contexts. My hope is that they provide a guide to help people think about how to take practical action in their own lives and churches and begin making the adjustments necessary to live in this new negative world reality as a moral minority. Again, the emphasis is on strengthening our own distinctiveness as the church while not neglecting and even strengthening our dedication to mission.

Not all my ideas are groundbreaking or radically new. Some of them are practices we should have already been doing but haven't taken hold. In the positive and neutral worlds, it was possible to get away with being lax—flying under the cultural radar. But in the negative world, that is no longer a viable position. So for some chapters I will highlight familiar areas where we already know what we need to do but now need to get far more serious about actually doing it.

WE CAN SUCCEED

One of the things I love about the Bible is its realism, how it's true to life. The Bible doesn't sugarcoat reality or the human condition. Similarly, Christians today should not ignore our cultural reality but rather be realistic about the negative world environment we live in. Yet recognizing the nature of our challenging environment doesn't mean we should become fatalistic or believe there's nothing we can do. We can do many things to start adapting to the negative world. There are ways for us to create churches that can thrive in this world. Perhaps outside pressure will catalyze the evangelical church in America to take our faith seriously in a way we never did before. New opportunities for evangelism will even present themselves because of the world's abandonment of truth.

The arrival of the negative world does not mean

evangelicalism is destined to suffer a slow death. Again, looking to the past, evangelicals have been nothing if not adaptable to changing times. Evangelicalism today is a product of prior successful adaptations to earlier stages of decline, and following the lead of our mighty and faithful God, we evangelicals can successfully adapt to this next phase.

PART TWO

LIVING

PERSONALLY

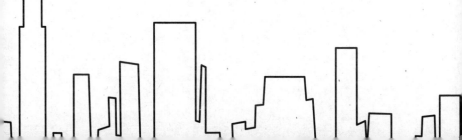

CHAPTER 4

BECOME OBEDIENT

INVESTOR WARREN BUFFETT FAMOUSLY SAID, "YOU only find out who is swimming naked when the tide goes out."[1] In a bull market, when the stock market is rising, it's easy for people to make money. During the dot-com boom in the late 1990s, for example, many venture capitalists looked like geniuses and, on paper at least, made fortunes investing in companies like Webvan and Pets.com. Hedge funds can make eye-popping returns in good times by investing with borrowed money. But when the market goes down, or there's a recession, or interest rates rise, it's a different story. Many of these supposedly great investors lose large amounts of money, and even major banks like Lehman Brothers or blue-chip manufacturers like General Motors sometimes go bankrupt.

Whether or not he knew it, Buffett was merely echoing what Jesus Christ said two thousand years ago. Jesus concluded his Sermon on the Mount with one of the most famous passages in Scripture:

> Everyone who hears these words of mine and puts them
> into practice is like a wise man who built his house on the

rock. The rain came down, the streams rose, and the winds blew and beat against that house; yet it did not fall, because it had its foundation on the rock. But everyone who hears these words of mine and does not put them into practice is like a foolish man who built his house on sand. The rain came down, the streams rose, and the winds blew and beat against that house, and it fell with a great crash. (Matthew 7:24–27)

In other words, only when the storm comes and the flood waters rise do we see the foundation on which we've built our lives and faith.

The positive and even neutral worlds might be compared to sunny weather for the Christian. It's true that we've never had a fully Christian or truly Christian society in the United States, and there have always been those who suffered and were persecuted for their faith. Yet at the same time, social rewards often went along with being known as a good churchgoing person. At a minimum there weren't many social penalties for a majority of people.

As we transition to the negative world, however, storm clouds have gathered on the horizon. How much rain will come and how high the flood waters might rise isn't yet known. But the possibility of a severe flood hitting our lives and faith is a real and tangible prospect in a way that it wasn't for most American evangelicals in past years.

The question we all face is whether our house is built on the Rock of Jesus Christ, or whether, despite our nominal professions of faith and our sitting in the pews of our churches every Sunday, our house of faith is built on nothing but sand. In Matthew 7, Jesus not only warns us how a flood will reveal the foundation of our faith but tells us how to build our house on the rock: *we hear his words and put them into practice.*

That is, for us to have lives built on a secure foundation, we must be obedient to Christ, to actually do what he told us to do.

This raises a question we must each ask ourselves: *How serious am I about doing what the Bible says?* We've read in and heard preached many instructions from Scripture—and many times. But have we considered the weight and significance of what they ask of us? For example, Jesus said we need to count the cost of our faith: "Suppose one of you wants to build a tower. Won't you first sit down and estimate the cost to see if you have enough money to complete it? For if you lay the foundation and are not able to finish it, everyone who sees it will ridicule you, saying, 'This person began to build and wasn't able to finish'" (Luke 14:28–30).

For many American evangelicals, life in a positive or neutral world meant they could breeze over these passages because the immediate cost of obedience or following what Jesus said was low or nonexistent. And as I've argued, for a majority of people, being a Christian came with secular, cultural benefits. How many of us ever considered whether our faith might cost us our job or was a barrier to advancement in our profession? That may not have been a cost for previous generations, but it seems possible today in a way that would have seemed impossible just twenty years ago.

In the past, when reading in the Bible about instructions to bear up while suffering unjustly or under persecution, perhaps some of us with no experience or history of that nodded our assent but with the assumption that it wasn't really applicable to our situation. Consider the apostle Paul writing to the Philippians about his blue-blood background and impeccable religious credentials, yet saying, "Whatever were gains to me I now consider loss for the sake of Christ. What is more, I consider everything a loss because of the surpassing worth of knowing Christ Jesus my Lord, for whose sake I have lost all things. I consider them garbage, that I may gain Christ" (Philippians 3:7–8).

Let's be honest. How many of us would legitimately count *all things* as loss for the sake of Christ? That was hard enough for Paul's original hearers to do, when life was, as the saying goes, nasty, brutish, and short. But the reality is that in twenty-first-century America, despite its many real problems, life can be pretty amazing for people with a middle-class or better income. Most American Christians have not been in danger of losing all they have for the sake of Christ.

When I lived just a five-minute walk from Central Park in New York City, I used to contemplate Paul's declaration in Philippians. I thought about what it would mean if I lost my job and had to leave the city, then lamented the potential loss of being able to take walks in the park. Even that thought—about a minor joy and comfort at the time—was difficult for me. I would like to think I'd be willing to pay whatever the price to follow Christ, but I have to admit that the idea of counting all things as loss for the sake of knowing Christ is aspirational for me—not a reality I've ever faced. And I don't think I'm alone in this.

Fortunately for us, the ultimate guarantor of our faith is Christ. Jesus told his disciples, for example, not to worry about what they would say when hauled into court, because the Spirit would give them utterance at the right time (Luke 21:12–15). Just before Peter was about to deny Jesus three times, Jesus prayed that his disciple's faith might not fail (Luke 22:31–36). When Peter was sinking beneath the waves, Jesus reached out and grabbed his hand to steady him (Matthew 14:31). We have a high priest who can sympathize with all our weaknesses (Hebrews 4:15–16).

Yet we're also promised that there will be difficulties and

tests of our faith. We're instructed to take action ourselves, and the Bible tells us that our willingness to obey Christ's commands is an outward sign of our inward faith (John 14:15). We should be "all in" when it comes to exercising faith by trusting the word of Christ and working hard to demonstrate that trust by obeying all of Jesus's commands. Then, as he himself said, we'll be building our lives on a sure foundation.

Other Scripture passages attest to similar concepts. Second Corinthians 7:1 says, "Let us purify ourselves from everything that contaminates body and spirit, perfecting holiness out of reverence for God." That is, we are to pursue holiness actively, seeking to cleanse ourselves of *every* defilement, not just the select ones we care about personally because they're causing problems in our lives.

Puritan writer John Owen, in his famous book *Mortification of Sin*, includes the pursuit of universal obedience to God's Word as one of only two pre-conditions, along with being saved, for being able to kill any sin. He writes,

> If you are trying with all your might to kill a sin or evil desire, why? It's causing you anxiety, it makes you afraid, you know it has bad consequences, and you don't feel like you have peace with God about it. But maybe you aren't praying and reading your Bible. Or maybe you've been committing other sins that aren't quite causing you as much personal trouble, but haven't done anything to kill them. Christ died for all these too. Why aren't you being diligent in killing all of your sin and carrying out all the duties you've been assigned? If you hate sin as sin then you would be just as aggressive about trying to stamp out all of it in your life. The fact that you are so selective in the particular sins you strive to defeat says plainly that the reason is because they are the only ones that are causing you pain and trouble. If

they weren't, you probably wouldn't be worried about them either. Now, do you think it likely God will put his seal of approval on your hypocrisy? Do you think He is going to provide relief in the sin that is particularly bothering you if you are going to go right along committing other sins that bother Him just as much?

Don't let anyone think he can do his own work if he won't do God's. God's work consists of *universal obedience*—obedience to God in everything. To be freed from only one sin—that's just our own agenda. That's why Paul says, "Let us purify ourselves from everything that contaminates body and spirit" (2 Corinthians 7:1). If we want to do anything, we have to do everything. So killing sin doesn't just come down to killing this or that evil desire. It involves a universally humble frame of heart, with watchfulness over every evil, along with the performance of every duty. That's what we must seek to do.[2]

In Acts 20:27 Paul said, "I have not hesitated to proclaim to you the whole will of God." That is, Paul intentionally sought to give people the totality of God's Word, not just a carefully curated selection of texts and teachings designed to appeal to a sophisticated Roman audience. Jesus warned his hearers of this as well, saying, "Anyone who sets aside one of the least of these commands and teaches others accordingly will be called least in the kingdom of heaven, but whoever practices and teaches these commands will be called great in the kingdom of heaven." (Matthew 5:19).

As tempting as it is for us to select some of his commands to obey and others to ignore, Jesus doesn't give us that option. The message is clear: we are to be "all in" on our faith, seeking to universally live out the Christian life in every place God has put us. Whenever the teachings of Christ and the demands of our culture conflict, we must be willing to pay a significant and tangible price to follow Christ.

In America, the time when people could "get along" as average or nominal Christians without actively pursuing spiritual growth and simply avoiding obvious and flagrant sin in their lives is coming to a close. Today, people are abandoning their faith, as seen, for example, in the growing decline of religious affiliation among young women.[3] And it's also occurring through an abandonment of orthodox doctrine, as has happened in some of the mainline churches over the past several decades.[4] As Paul warned, "The time will come when people will not put up with sound doctrine" (2 Timothy 4:3).

Today's world allows people to be accepted while identifying as Christian *if they bring their doctrine into alignment with the world's standards.* This pull toward compromise to be culturally accepted creates a fertile environment for the abandonment of orthodoxy. As Jesus said to the church at Laodicea, "I know your deeds, that you are neither cold nor hot. I wish you were either one or the other! So, because you are lukewarm—neither hot nor cold—I am about to spit you out of my mouth" (Revelation 3:15–16).

As I noted in the introduction, I am neither a pastor nor a theologian. This is a book of cultural analysis, not Bible teaching. But in speaking to Christians about emerging challenges in uncertain times, I can't limit myself to purely secular strategies when more fundamental spiritual problems exist. As many have said, the gospel is not good advice of the type you might get from a strategy consultant; it's good news. And the ultimate rock of our life, the ultimate object of our faith in a negative world, must be Jesus Christ.

The first challenge for American evangelicals living in the negative world, then, is to examine ourselves, consider our ways, count the cost, and commit to denying ourselves, taking up our crosses and following Christ in everything. This must happen no matter what the price, confident that Jesus will never fail us or forsake us, that all things will work together for our good, and that whatever suffering we do endure in this world is not worthy to be compared with the glory to be revealed in the age to come.

If we aren't solid in our faith, nothing else we do will ultimately be of any consequence. We have to be fully committed to our faith and obedient to Jesus's words as he himself said in the Sermon on the Mount. We must train our hearts and minds to hear his words and then do what they say. As the well-known hymn reminds us, on Christ the solid rock we stand, all other ground is sinking sand.[5]

CHAPTER 5

BECOME EXCELLENT

EVANGELICAL HISTORIAN MARK NOLL'S BOOK
The Scandal of the Evangelical Mind was published in 1994.
The scandal, in his view, was that evangelicals didn't seem to
have much of a mind. That is, they were incapable of applying genuinely Christian thought to the intellectual domains of
society. This, he offered, was because of some of their belief
systems, such as dispensationalism, and a lack of institutional
support for intellectual work.

A lack of worldly intellectual bona fides isn't always a bad
thing. After all, Paul said God chose the foolish things of the
world to confound the wise (1 Corinthians 1:27). And many
of the groups Noll criticized for their anti-intellectual attitudes
had other important virtues, as he himself made sure to stress
in his book. The fundamentalists positively exemplified the
power of a simple faith and a willingness to hold to the truth in
the face of opposition. Their attitude of "God said it, I believe
it, and that settles it" enabled them to retain belief in the doctrines of the virgin birth, the bodily resurrection of Christ
from the dead, and the historicity of miracles when the leading
scholars of the day scoffed at and mocked them.

And Pentecostalism, though often criticized for being anti-intellectual, is one of the fastest growing Christian movements in the world because it speaks to and helps people whose bondage to sin is tangible, not just intellectual. Many of their ministries have helped people like the opioid addict and the ex-con experience freedom from bondage to sin. Those in this tradition may know viscerally what many sophisticated people grasp only theoretically—that sin kills, and only the power of the Holy Spirit can break the chains of sin.

Even among evangelicals who have intellectual credentials, some who possess the most expertise in a particular field sometimes demonstrate little evidence of how Christianity informs their work. World-class scientist Francis Collins, the evangelical former director of the National Institutes of Health and the National Center for the Human Genome Project, oversaw the funding of experiments using tissue from aborted babies[1] and explicitly endorsed a panoply of secular progressive social views.[2] It's not immediately obvious how his Christian convictions affected his leadership of the NIH or if that institution would have been run materially differently with a non-Christian at the helm.

Excellence, intellectual or otherwise, is not the same as godliness, yet it should be a goal we pursue. We can be godly—pursuing holiness, being obedient to Christ, evangelizing our neighbors, and caring for the poor—while also cultivating excellence in all that we do, including the intellectual life of the mind.

Three decades after Noll's book was published, the challenge of developing an evangelical intellectualism remains. Tim Keller revisited this topic in a series on renewing the American evangelical church, where he listed seven areas he sees as critical to this task of renewal. One of them is what he calls the "Christian mind project." He wrote,

Evangelicalism has a strongly anti-intellectual cast to it that must be overcome without losing its appeal to the majority of the population. The goals include increasing the number of Christians on faculties, forging a robust intellectual culture for orthodox Protestantism, and increasing the number of Christian public intellectuals. This will not only entail promoting believers into the existing intellectual and cultural economy of basically (a) largely progressive universities and (b) largely conservative think tanks. It will also mean creating some kind of alternate cultural economy for scholarship and intellectual work.[3]

This need for evangelical intellectual development goes beyond academic scholarship and its corresponding institutions, though it certainly includes them. It also involves improving evangelical performance and aspirations in a variety of other vocational domains.

Think about a common, everyday area like physical fitness. Many websites are devoted to physical fitness, yet few of them are written by people who appear to be Christian, and the advice they dole out is clearly from a non-Christian perspective. This doesn't mean there's a need for an "evangelical body builder bro." Rather, what's needed are people who can provide truly excellent information about health and fitness while presenting it in a manner informed by a Christian view of life—as part of stewarding our bodies, of being healthy and strong enough to be a blessing to the world, and of not pursuing personal health because of vanity or for the purpose of increasing one's chances to fornicate or engage in other immoral activity.

This example could be repeated in many other domains as well. With the exception of a few areas like public speaking (for example, preaching) and marketing, where some evangelicals are truly world-class, evangelicals don't typically value or pursue genuine *excellence*, nor do they assert institutional or professional leadership. This needs to change.

Keller, too, calls for more than simply intellectualism, referencing the development of his longstanding priority of integrating faith and work. He also asks us to imagine "an increasing number of Christian artists—working out both the realism of the Christian worldview about sin and the confident expectation of restorative grace—produce high-quality stories, music, and visual art."[4] I don't claim Keller's endorsement for my thoughts here but simply want to highlight that from Noll's book published three decades ago to Tim Keller's challenge to renew the church today, the lack of excellence in the evangelical church has been recognized as a problem.

This lack of excellence and expertise has tremendous implications for the evangelical world. Since the mid-1980s, evangelicals have overwhelmingly identified as politically conservative and voted Republican, and though they are a moral minority in this country today, they arguably remain the largest and most important voting bloc in the Republican Party. Yet evangelicals are almost entirely absent from the senior leadership positions of major conservative think tanks and publications.[5] As of 2022, the majority of leaders at these institutions were Catholic or Jewish, with any Protestant leaders being Episcopalian except for one lone evangelical.[6]

Movement conservatism has had a Catholic slant since the time William F. Buckley Jr. founded *National Review* in 1955, so one might argue conservatism has a pro-Catholic bias.[7] But by and large, evangelicals haven't developed the skills necessary for nor had the orientation toward obtaining leadership positions in these kinds of organizations.

Something similar is on display in the legal world, where evangelicals have been famously absent from the Supreme

Court.[8] We also see that in other key areas, evangelicals often find themselves looking to Catholic intellectuals, even ones who are critical of Protestantism, to understand key aspects of our world. This is evident in Protestant appropriation of insights, such as Charles Taylor on secularization[9] and Patrick Deneen on liberalism.[10]

Obviously, there is nothing wrong with engaging with traditions other than our own, and it should even be encouraged. My point is that evangelicals tend to lack a presence in these areas, and until this improves, we will remain in a subordinate role with our agenda and much of our understanding of the world set by those outside evangelicalism.

SOCIETY'S REJECTION
OF NATURAL LAW

Even more so in today's negative world than when Mark Noll wrote his book on the scandal of the evangelical mind, it's necessary for evangelicals to develop and sustain our own intellectual resources at the highest levels. That's because the secular individuals in many of these fields and the institutions they control are now rejecting not just the specifically Christian beliefs liberal Protestantism rejected, but many of Christianity's core ethical and moral principles as well. In many cases, they are now at war not just with Christian dogma but with the created order of the universe itself.

Joe Rigney, former president of Bethlehem College and Seminary, highlights this in his own view of the dangers posed to Christians in the negative world.[11] He notes that elite society had long rejected many of the "peculiar doctrines of Christianity,"[12] such as the virgin birth, yet accepted what C. S. Lewis referred to as "the Tao" in his book *The Abolition of Man*. The Tao is a Chinese concept referring to the natural order of the universe, often grasped intuitively rather than deductively.[13] Lewis used this Chinese word to illustrate the truly cross-cultural nature of this order created by God, which we in the West have often referred to as natural law or general revelation.

This is what Paul was referring to in Romans 1:20: "Since the creation of the world God's invisible qualities—his eternal power and divine nature—have been clearly seen, being understood from what has been made, so that people are without excuse." Everyone is capable of apprehending God's created order in the universe, which includes ethical and moral principles such as honoring your father and mother and not murdering others. Even atheists know and assert that murder is wrong. And even Thomas Jefferson, an intellectual suspicious of the miraculous, found much of moral and ethical value in the Bible.

Not every culture discerned or followed the Tao equally or in every respect. And it's not possible to fully apprehend God's designs without his specific revelations in the Bible. But there was broad, nearly universal agreement on many shared principles, a number of which C. S. Lewis listed in his book.

While twentieth-century liberal Protestants rejected the supernatural elements of Christianity, they largely held to the natural law and moral structures of Christianity. Famed liberal preacher Harry Emerson Fosdick, for example, held traditional Christian views on sexuality that would be seen as retrograde today. He rejected adultery and homosexuality, and he even playfully mocked the idea that children might believe they are the opposite sex as a childhood fantasy.[14]

Rigney argues that what is unique about the negative world is that it involves not just a rejection of Christianity and its "peculiar" doctrines but also a rejection of parts of the Tao, a rejection of the created order of the world. For example, not only have nearly universal notions about the family been rejected, but even the biological reality of gender as well. Increasingly, remaining a member in good standing in polite society requires affirming absurd positions. One is simultaneously believing that gender is completely a social construct *and* that someone identifying as other than their biological sex at a physical and metaphysical level is their claimed gender. This is a clear case of cognitive dissonance.

Not all of the natural law is rejected, though. Again, murder is still mostly regarded as wrong, for example. Nor is our society devoid of law entirely. Indeed, if anything, society is highly legalistic and harsh if one transgresses the rules of the new social morality. As previously noted, philosopher Chantal Delsol calls this a "normative inversion" in select areas. There's a new secular moral law that's often at odds with natural law.

This rejection of the Tao heightens both the challenges evangelicalism faces in seeking excellence and the stakes if we fail in the negative world. Not only are the leadership classes of our society rejecting Christian-specific doctrines, but many are also rejecting the broad moral and ethical framework once largely shared between mainline and evangelical Christianity. This rejection is often given with intellectual or "scientific" justifications.

For Christians today, the intellectual leaders of our society are far less reliable and trustworthy than they once were. Lacking a shared understanding of reality and the moral order, evangelicals can no longer rely on their wisdom or defer to their judgments.

REASONS FOR EVANGELICALS
TO PURSUE EXCELLENCE

In a negative world where Christians increasingly find themselves excluded from elite positions in many domains or forced
to suppress their Christian views if allowed in, you might
assume the need for excellence would be lessened. A strategy of
encouraging more Christians to become professors in secular
colleges and universities might have made sense in a positive or
a neutral world, but in a negative world, why bother?

And there is a sense in which this is true. The influence of
Christians in these institutions and their ability to bring transformation to them may be significantly limited. Those who
speak out may lose their position. But it's important to adopt
a broader perspective on this matter, and I believe there are
many good reasons why it's necessary for Christians to pursue
this kind of influence and value excellence.

First, it's necessary to have Christians in these institutions
and with these skills if we're to have any hope of evangelizing intellectuals and elites in our society today. Paul himself
came from an intellectually elite background, and he never
stopped trying to reach the elites of his day, whether they were
the governors of Judea, the Praetorian Guard, or those on the
Areopagus in Athens. Christ attracted the humble and lowly,
but also Nicodemus and Joseph of Arimathea, leaders of the
Jewish religious establishment. The Great Commission extends
to all levels of society.

In fact, one of the great aims of the cultural engagement
movement (which, not coincidentally, emerged in the period
following Noll's book) is that it sought to intentionally reach
and evangelize people in these spheres of influence. While it
largely failed to reach those at the very top levels of most fields
and did not lead to cultural transformation on a widespread

scale, it showed a respect for the life of the mind and genuine excellence. And this commitment to reaching people at every level of society and pursuing excellence for the sake of Christ are still worthy goals we should not abandon even in the negative world and regardless of whether they ever lead to cultural transformation and change.

Second, the pursuit of intellectual excellence is necessary for the purposes of counter-catechesis. I return to this in chapter 8, but the church today not only has to teach its members and next generations what it believes, but explain why it doesn't believe certain doctrines accepted in the world. This will require not just saying that these positions are morally wrong, but in many cases intellectually discrediting them as well. We need indigenous leaders who can serve as intellectual guides in a world where the secular elites reject not only Christ but, as Rigney noted, Christianity's ethical and moral principles and the created order of the world as well.

Not all secular science or leadership is corrupted today, but where truth comes into conflict with secular ideologies, these ideologies win most of the time. That's true even if they are denying basic biological facts. As impossible as this might seem, keep in mind that this is what we saw, even in the supposedly hard sciences, in the Soviet Union, when the genetic basis of inherited traits was rejected in favor of ideologically derived explanations.[15]

Third, it's important to pursue intellectual excellence to have the skills, including the exploration and startup-type skills, necessary to develop strategies for living in the negative world and to successfully navigate our own churches and institutions through an uncertain, dynamic future. For example, as a preview of a topic I return to in greater depth in chapter 10, we need to develop a more sophisticated approach to gender and family fit for today's industrial society. There is a lot of work still to be done in many areas.

Fourth, we need to pursue excellence because evangelicals who do find themselves leading major institutions or in key positions need to be prepared to do a first-rate job. This is especially true in the political realm, where it's likely that many evangelicals will still be elected even well into the negative world. And it's possible that an evangelical might, if they developed the skills and orientation, be named the president of a major conservative think tank, for example. Evangelicals need to cultivate and develop people who are ready to assume these roles.

Yet existing evangelical culture renders its people largely incapable of leading and shaping major institutions and domains of society. Even where evangelicals are heavily represented in a domain, like American political conservatism, they typically don't lead it. And when they do rise to those top positions, they often don't have the mindset or skills that would allow them to truly transform those domains. Instead, they tend to conform to the existing institutional culture rather than transform it.

Finally, it will simply be more difficult to visibly live as a Christian in American society going forward. This means that the average lay member of an evangelical church will need to seek excellence in their life, understanding what it means to be distinctively Christian in their ordinary callings, such as spouse or parent. Christian life in the negative world will require more intentionality, focus, and effort than before.

THE SOCIOECONOMIC STRATIFICATION OF PROTESTANTISM

Why have evangelicals long been deficient in intellectualism, the arts, and sciences? Why have we not cultivated excellence? Without knowing what the problem is, it's hard to suggest a solution.

Evangelical anti-intellectualism and the lack of elite skills and orientations in domains like the arts or institutional leadership result in part from the stratified nature of Protestantism in the United States. In 1958 the late sociologist E. Digby Baltzell, the foremost American scholar of the American upper-class WASP establishment, contrasted Protestantism with Catholicism this way:

> One of the important consequences of the Reformation has been the fact that whereas the Catholic Church traditionally ministered to all social strata, the numerous Protestant sects and denominations have been divided along class lines virtually from the beginning. Today, while each individual Protestant congregation tends towards class homogeneity, the Catholic parish, larger in size and geographically organized, ministers to the whole community.[16]

Baltzell perhaps understates the degree to which Catholicism in the US was ethnically partitioned across different parishes, but nevertheless, Catholicism was able to incorporate more diversity within its unified structure than Protestant denominations were. This included not just ethnic diversity but also various currents of reform or sensibility. Baltzell, himself a WASP, described it this way in his 1979 book *Puritan Boston and Quaker Philadelphia*:

> In striking contrast to Protestantism's endless exclusiveness and the consequent spawning of sects in every generation, the genius of Catholicism has been its ability to include, in each generation, both old and new truths, eventually absorbing the new into the old in a novel synthesis. This inclusiveness was made possible by an elitist and hierarchical ethic based on a double standard of morality. The spiritual elite, rather

than breaking away in a sectarian schism, voluntarily joined a monastic order based on a perfectionist ideal. Most orders were founded not by the official hierarchy but by a perfectionist layman or priest who, in the interest of some new truth, was usually branded a heretic. Thus, the order and the sect were commonly founded by members of discontented classes, often making a strong appeal to women (both the Franciscans and the Quakers received enthusiastic support from female servants). Unlike Protestantism, the Catholic church eventually absorbed and institutionalized the new truths and their propagators.[17]

Protestantism was, in essence, the reform movement that the Catholic Church was unable to contain within it, as their theological and political differences proved irreconcilable. Protestantism itself then continued to be highly fractious and prone to division. In the US, these divisions stratified the church racially and shamefully with regard to blacks, and in some cases ethnically, as with the Lutherans, and also socioeconomically.

One result of the socioeconomic stratification is that in the past it wasn't uncommon for people to change denominations as they moved up in society. Baltzell described the process like this, quoting a Jesuit:

> The average American is born the son of a Baptist or Methodist farmer; after obtaining an education he becomes a businessman in a large city where he joins a suburban, Presbyterian church; finally, upon achieving the acme of economic success, he joins a fashionable Episcopal church in order to satisfy his wife's social ambitions.[18]

Of course, not all upwardly mobile people changed denominations. John D. Rockefeller remained a staunch Baptist, for example. But many did. Note that this change almost always involved conversion into the more prestigious mainline denominations and away from denominations associated with fundamentalism and evangelicalism. In fact, this inbound flow of new members from among the upwardly mobile played a key role in sustaining the mainline denominations. When this went away, it was one of the factors leading to the decline of those denominations.[19]

Because of this stratification, Protestants who had the expertise and status to operate at the highest levels of society as intellectuals, artists, scholars, executives, and major institutional leaders ended up disproportionately concentrated in the top-tier mainline denominations. And they often used major mainstream universities or other institutions as their home base.

The religion of elite Episcopalians or Presbyterians was often liberal Protestantism of a type decried by evangelicals both then and now. Nevertheless, through them, Protestant Christianity found public expression. And the values of that liberal Protestantism, which included ethical principles largely shared with evangelicals, heavily shaped the character of the WASP establishment.

US Secretary of State John Foster Dulles, who served in President Eisenhower's administration in the 1950s and for whom the eponymous Washington, DC, airport is named, was the son of a Presbyterian minister and an active churchman on the modernist side of the fundamentalist-modernist controversy. In his religious biography of Dulles, John D. Wilsey said of him, "Foster's religious life as it animated his career as lawyer, churchman, and diplomat can be summed up as a blend of exceptionalist civil religion and progressive Christianity."[20] While Dulles's theology may be alien to an evangelical, he brought a set of intellectual and social skills to the table many evangelicals of his day did not possess.

For example, he negotiated a peace treaty with forty-nine countries that formally ended the war with Japan, and later as Secretary of State under President Eisenhower, he put in place several other key treaties. Dulles and mainline lay business and civic leaders like him were capable of conducting affairs at high levels among social and political elites, and they had the confidence to create and reshape institutions and society to fit changing times. More explicitly religious thinkers like Reinhold Niebuhr were respected public intellectuals as well.

Those with higher level intellectual or social skills and an orientation toward leadership largely found themselves attracted to and formed within this mainline tradition or a parallel Catholic one. Evangelicals lacked this intellectual and leadership tradition, and to the extent that someone of evangelical background developed in this direction, they would quickly, as the saying goes, move on up. Nevertheless, this mainline tradition provided a Protestant intellectual and leadership perspective and culture that was of high value to society. The decline of the mainline religious tradition is part of what plagues our society and is partially responsible for today's widely lamented leadership deficit.

Evangelicals have been incapable of filling the gap in leading and shaping major institutions and domains of society. Again, even where they're heavily represented in a domain, like American political conservatism, they don't lead it. With the decline of mainline denominations, this has left a Protestant leadership void in society outside select domains like the business world.

CREATING A CULTURE OF EXCELLENCE

Building a culture that nurtures and values excellence will not be easy. From its origins, evangelicalism has been a middle-class movement, possessing a breadth that has successfully reached many millions of people with the gospel. But as a middle-class movement, it's traditionally lacked access to the elite centers of education, politics, and other cultural domains. By definition, a focus on the middle means you're essentially average.

Evangelicalism has always had strong populist currents, and anti-elitism is part of the populist DNA and played a key role in shaping the evangelical world. In recent years, it helps explain the draw of evangelicals to Donald Trump, for example, who makes it a habit of regularly bashing American elites. The pursuit of excellence is by its very nature a form of elite orientation, and evangelicals tend to be uncomfortable with the very idea of elite-ness even though every society and every institution has elites.

Would it not be far better for those elites to be Christian and represent a Christian mindset and perspective? A lack of social orientation toward institutional leadership has meant that evangelicals have effectively ceded leadership in society to people who don't share their values. Wherever the culture of evangelicalism has been inhospitable to the pursuit of excellence, those evangelicals who do desire excellence often end up defecting from the movement. If they don't leave the Christian faith and defect to secularism itself, they often convert to mainline Protestant Christianity, Catholicism, or Eastern Orthodoxy.[21]

Countering these ongoing defections away from the evangelical fold will necessitate the creation of space within evangelicalism for the pursuit of excellence in intellectual endeavors, the arts, sciences, medicine, law, and institutional leadership, much in the same way the Catholic Church has done. Evangelicalism must seek a way to overcome the socioeconomic stratification that has long plagued American Protestantism, if for no other reason than to be able to carry the Great Commission into every part of society.

Evangelicals will also need to find a way to extend the culture of excellence as it develops within the evangelical church from the true geniuses to the average person in the pews. Life in twenty-first-century America is simply harder than it was in the twentieth century. The middle class that formed the social base of evangelicalism is being hollowed out as we become more of a two-tier society—a world where, as economist Tyler Cowen put it, "average is over."[22]

It's far more difficult to be a faithful and successful Christian husband or wife in a society where divorce is praised and accepted as the norm. It's hard to raise up godly Christian children in today's environment or to provide for a family while not stepping on one of secular society's land mines. It's not easy pastoring a church today. But when times are tough, everyone needs to elevate their game.

We can't afford to wait around for this to happen at the institutional level, though we should continue efforts there as well. Many of the near-term actions we can take are more personal and individually oriented. It starts with each one of us committing to cultivating excellence in whatever we do. God has placed each one of us into a particular place in life for this time. He's given each of us different talents, but everyone has received some gifts from God (1 Corinthians 12:8–9). Whatever gifts we've been given, we'll be held accountable for how we develop them and use them to bear fruit for the kingdom. As stewards of the grace of God, we need to pursue excellence as we develop those gifts and use the resources God has entrusted to us, from the life of the mind to effective, godly parenting.

CHAPTER 6

BECOME RESILIENT

EARLY CHRISTIANS OFTEN EXPERIENCED EXTREME physical persecution, including torture and death. Today, Christians in many countries face similar risk of being physically attacked, imprisoned, or even killed. Christians in North Korea or China experience trials that likely parallel some of the persecution early New Testament Christians faced.

While there have been forms of physical persecution against some Christians in the United States at times—notably those in the black church and some in the Catholic Church—for the most part American Christians don't suffer that kind of persecution and hopefully never will even in the negative world. But that doesn't mean Christians never face significant challenges. Modern technological society provides many ways to impose indirect, subtle, and virtual pressures on people, ways that did not exist in the preindustrial society of the New Testament. Paul was shipwrecked, stoned, beaten with rods, and imprisoned, but as far as we know, no one ever took away his ability to support himself as a tentmaker.

In America today, not only Christians but many people face a variety of social and economic risks if they run afoul of the new public ideological line. For example, everyone is at risk of being the target of a social media hate storm. In one famous case, Justine Sacco, an ordinary person with only 170 Twitter followers, made a joke about South Africa that went viral under the hashtag #hasjustinelandedyet while she was on a flight to that country. By the time her flight landed, she'd been fired from her job, and her name is now permanently associated with this incident.[1]

People who work in a corporate job have good reason to fear they might lose their job if they say the wrong thing or decline to participate in employer social initiatives that conflict with their conscience.[2] Some may randomly become the target of an online outrage mob. Though unlikely, it's both possible and possible in a way that it wasn't in the past.

It's relatively easy to be suspended or banned from social media. Twitter, for example, regularly suspended users for "deadnaming" or "misgendering" transgendered people.[3] This has happened to even high-profile people like a sitting US Congressman.[4] With social media serving as the largest and most visible public square today, being banned from these platforms is tantamount to being silenced or exiled from public discussion. Though relatively few people have been permanently banned from these platforms, when this is a real possibility, it inculcates some level of fear in the public.

A recent *New York Times*/Siena College poll found that 55 percent of Americans have personally held back from speaking freely out of fear.[5] And 84 percent of respondents believed that people not being able to speak freely is a problem in this country. And it's not just Christians who have a growing fear they will transgress the new ideological lines and believe that America is becoming a less free country. These surveys indicate a real threat, not evangelical paranoia.

UNDERSTANDING REAL-WORLD RISK

As evangelicals face the more hostile environment of the negative world, they can no longer rely on an underlying friendliness or even neutrality when they interact with social institutions. But rather than live in fear, we should be intentionally structuring our lives to be more resilient in the face of hostile actions by these institutions. This resiliency will reduce the downside risk from falling afoul of secular culture and buffer believers against the pressure to compromise on biblical teachings. In addition, it will enable us to reject fear and lead to greater boldness in mission and evangelism.

This restructuring first requires an understanding of how to think about and manage risk. Former options trader and author Nassim Taleb, who also has a PhD in mathematics, has long focused on managing real-world risk. In his 2007 bestselling book *The Black Swan*, he strongly disagreed with high-profile analysts, including a future Nobel Prize–winning economist, about the risks faced by government-sponsored mortgage guarantors Fannie Mae and Freddie Mac. They claimed these entities were safe, while Taleb contended they were not safe at all and were in fact quite risky.[6] Shortly thereafter, Taleb was proven right when in 2008 Fannie and Freddie went bankrupt and were put into federal receivership in the wake of the financial crash.[7] That his prophetic warnings proved true helped make the book a bestseller and Taleb something of an intellectual celebrity.

Taleb has laid out his ideas on managing risk in a series of five books he calls the Incerto.[8] He argues that one of the greatest factors driving success or failure is random chance, or luck. Very successful people may be smart and hardworking, but the distinguishing characteristic behind their outsized success is luck. He used the book *The Millionaire Next Door* as an illustration of the kinds of naive and false explanations given for how rich people get rich.[9] He contends that simply looking at successful people's actions and then extrapolating lessons from what they did is subject to "survivorship bias." For example, the authors of *The Millionaire Next Door* looked at millionaires to see what they had in common, but they didn't examine the people who did the very same things yet ended up far less wealthy—or even bankrupt. By definition, the method excluded failures from the sample. And the larger the population size, the greater the risk of falling prey to survivorship bias. In a large country like the United States, for example, even random chance will produce many millionaires.

Although I'm not a millionaire, my own life confirms this bias. I will readily acknowledge that whatever success I've personally had in life is primarily the result of good fortune. I'm intelligent, but that intelligence is innate; I didn't do anything to produce it. It's like winning the lottery. Similarly, I had a good upbringing, but I did nothing to select the home, community, or church environment I was raised in. That was also random from my perspective. I met my wife at a church I visited only three or four times, and one of those times a mutual acquaintance decided to introduce us. What were the odds of that happening? I could go on and on, as many other significant and life-altering happenings in my life were due to seemingly random events. Or at least I did very little to nothing to make them happen.

Another Taleb concept is what he calls a "black swan" event. Black swans are rare, unpredictable events that have an outsized effect on outcomes. They're impossible to predict in advance but seem obvious and sometimes inevitable in retrospect. An example of a black swan event is the 9/11 terrorist attacks.[10]

When you combine randomness and black swans, the result is a world largely governed by chance, where the outcomes are heavily driven by a few extreme outlier events that can't be predicted. This doesn't seem right to most of us, but consider the events of the last few years.

On January 1, 2015, roughly two years before he was inaugurated as president, who would have imagined that Donald Trump would be the next president of the United States? Or think back to Christmas 2019. How many people imagined that the new year would bring a pandemic that would radically upend life all around the world? How many people thought there would be a Russian attack on Ukraine in 2022 that would send energy prices soaring, especially in Europe?

It's easy, in retrospect, to find events that intuitively validate Taleb's claims. Things we never imagined—the "unknown unknowns" as former Defense Secretary Donald Rumsfeld once famously called them[11]—have a huge impact on our world and our lives.

The dominance of randomness and extreme events in determining outcomes is at odds with our own high view of human agency and sense of control over our own lives. It's difficult for humans to understand and apply because it's difficult to accept. It's contrary to how we think and act.

It also doesn't seem very Christian, does it? Yet if we make two vocabulary substitutions, we can translate Taleb's claims into a Christian way of thinking. The first is to replace his concept of "randomness" with "the sovereignty of God." And the second is to replace "black swan" with "room for God to show up, in ways we can't even imagine." In other words, while we as Christians don't believe this world is governed by the schemes of man or random chance, we do believe it's ultimately subject to the sovereignty of an almighty God, who uses even the chaos and evil of this world to accomplish his will and purposes and works all things together for our good (Romans 8:28).

This is not to suggest that God's actions are or even appear to be random. But even what seem like random events to us are subject to his sovereignty. And no circumstances in our world limit his ability to act, including in ways we can't even imagine, as numerous Scriptures attest. For example, 1 Samuel 14:6 says, "Nothing can hinder the LORD from saving, whether by many or by few," and Ephesians 3:20 tells us God is "able to do immeasurably more than all we ask or imagine."

So while we can translate Taleb's arguments into our Christian understanding of reality, for clarity and consistency I continue using his language of randomness and the black swan concept throughout the rest of this chapter.

LIVING IN A WORLD OF RISK

How should we structure our lives in light of the importance of randomness and unpredictable extreme events? Or to put this another way, how should evangelicals act if we're always exposed to some form of risk of bad things happening to us, even if the risk is small? How should we live if there's always the possibility of social rejection or being fired from our job for our Christian beliefs?

We have obvious biblical answers—walking by faith in God's promises, being watchful and alert, and always praying— but I want to focus on a practical strategy for structuring our lives in a negative world, a culture that sees Christian beliefs negatively and suspiciously.

One answer is to restructure our lives to reduce our exposure to risk from negative events and black swans. We should work to be resilient when faced with these negative shocks and potentially even gain from negative events. Taleb calls this being "antifragile."[12]

The early church is a good example of what it means to live in this antifragile way of life. It grew, and even grew stronger, from the persecution it suffered. Persecution in and of itself is not a good thing, as it involves individuals committing grave evils. And it may not always strengthen the church, but it did then. My goal in suggesting that evangelical Christians develop resiliency is not about trying to predict events or negative shocks. Again, this is generally impossible. Rather, the goal is to reduce our risk exposure and be positioned to survive or even benefit from these negative events.

If we want to be "antifragile" and possess a resilient strength, the first question is to ask what creates fragility. Being too big can make some things fragile, as was the case with the dinosaurs, who were wiped out in an asteroid collision while much smaller mammals survived.[13] A lack of redundancy can also create fragility, which is one reason God gave us two of many of our critical organs, like kidneys and lungs. Overoptimizing for efficiency can also create fragility, as does complexity.[14] We saw this on display in the supply chain disruptions during the COVID-19 pandemic. In all these cases, reducing the sources of fragility increases resilience and leaves the system or organism better equipped to face external shocks.

For example, the lens of fragility is one way we can explain the stunning collapse of Mars Hill Church in Seattle. Mars Hill was once one of the largest, fastest growing, and highest profile churches in America, with several locations and as many as fourteen thousand attendees.[15] But its large size and dependence on a single celebrity pastor, Mark Driscoll, led it to rapidly implode when he became embroiled in scandal.[16] Any megachurch is similarly vulnerable to a crisis of confidence in which large numbers of members exit. Even something seemingly innocuous like the retirement of a high-profile pastor can create transition challenges for large institutions.

FINANCIAL FRUGALITY

While resilience and antifragility are important when considering institutions, my focus in this chapter is about structuring our individual and family lives. And a key source of potential household fragility is finances. High levels of debt, a lack of savings, an outsized lifestyle, and dependence on elite institutions (like Fortune 500 companies) for jobs all increase risk exposure and fragility. By contrast, avoiding these things increases one's resilience. By moving toward genuine financial independence, an individual becomes more antifragile. Financial independence not only gives people more time to invest in God's mission but enables them to be bold and take risks for the sake of that mission. And while not everyone can become fully financially independent to the point of being antifragile, most people can at least become more financially resilient.

Christian financial advisor Dave Ramsey has long advocated getting and staying out of debt. He provides a number of helpful techniques and tools that have enabled many people to accomplish greater financial resiliency.[17] Other models for thinking about personal finances are offered as well. One of the most intriguing is a movement called Financial Independence, Retire Early (FIRE) that has become increasingly popular among millennials. Several websites are devoted to the movement, often published under colorful names like "Mr. Money Mustache."[18]

Those pursuing the FIRE approach deliberately embrace an ultra-lean lifestyle in order to save the majority of their income, in some cases as much as 70 percent. Doing this has allowed some individuals to retire in their thirties with a million dollars or more in the bank.[19] Those who pursue a FIRE lifestyle are often employed in technology or other higher paying fields of work, making rapidly saving a substantial amount of money feasible.

The FIRE strategy enables two powerful realities for negative world Christians. First, even a few years of savings can provide a significant cash cushion to serve as a form of "cancellation insurance." It provides the security they need while finding another job if they've been fired for their beliefs, for example, or even laid off because of an economic downturn. Of course, working hard to build a significant pool of savings will accomplish this whether or not a person is pursuing the full FIRE strategy. And realistically, most people won't be able to do that. My own family isn't following this lifestyle, yet the concepts behind it and the tips for how to save money are still helpful for many people. They're widely available on FIRE-focused blogs online.

There's also a second benefit to pursuing financial independence, or at least a conservative financial posture, for the negative world Christian. Taleb notes that one way to create an antifragile position is through a "barbell strategy," with a large safe position at one end and a riskier position or collection of smaller riskier positions at the other.[20] Achieving financial independence creates the safe position that allows a person to then take on significantly greater risk in a difficult negative world environment for the sake of Christian mission (or whatever activity they feel called to do).

The point of this is not to use our financial independence to, as pastor John Piper once said in a well-known sermon, spend time collecting seashells.[21] Rather, it's to free Christians to a more dedicated and bold pursuit of mission.

The Bubp family adopted the FIRE technique to do just that.[22] Ken Bubp and his wife started living frugally to pay off their student loans. Providentially, they discovered the FIRE community online and realized that if they saved half or more of their income and invested it, they could reach financial independence in their forties rather than waiting until their seventies.

As they shared, "This was a bolt from the blue." Bubp is now "retired" in his forties and describes his family's path:

> We lived on something less than half of our combined modest income. (For most of that time I worked at a non-profit; my wife was a teacher before stepping out to care for our two kids.) We bought a perfectly nice but modest older home. We tithed and were generous beyond that. We invested the remainder in low-cost index funds. We never felt we were deprived. In fact, we found ourselves freer even along the way than some of our friends who were borrowing money to fill their too-big and over-leveraged homes. We never thought we were doing anything heroic. In fact, it seemed joyfully simple. Just under ten years after paying off that debt and starting our family, we reached financial independence where we could live entirely off of our investments if needed. I quit my job and entered a work-optional life.[23]

Bubp notes that this approach has freed him to be bolder and take more risks, as he is no longer beholden to being employed to pay his bills. Since "retiring," he's volunteered to help a friend launch a national nonprofit, done some paid consulting work, volunteered at his church in a part-time capacity while his pastor was on sabbatical, and worked with a friend to help launch a music festival in his town. He's also effectively cancel-proof. As he said to me, "Being 'canceled' *might* be painful in some other ways, but it will not threaten my income."

To be clear, realistically, I know most people won't achieve financial independence or retire in their forties. I certainly didn't. The concept of saving a significant share of our income is mostly applicable to higher income households. But all of us can take small steps to implement a more conservative financial structure, one that leads to more savings and creates resiliency in the face of negative world risks.[24] And those with lower incomes have probably already reduced their ideological risk exposure because they likely don't work in the high-status domains where people are most exposed to the risk of being fired or paying some other price for holding a socially disapproved opinion.

This is simple, practical wisdom that can give us more space to confidently engage in mission even in a negative world. Will everyone be able to do this? No. But is it wise to seek it if we're able? Yes. And that is especially true in a world opposed to Christian beliefs. Tentmaking strategies and financial independence enable greater freedom to pursue God's purposes.

CAREER, FAMILY, AND GEOGRAPHY

This chapter is focused on developing resilience, and doing this with our finances is just one of many ways to pursue resilience. The same considerations that drive our financial decisions can also be relevant to other major life choices. For example, by their very nature, certain careers have more risk exposure than others. Working in a Fortune 500–type corporate environment or in a highly regulated profession like medicine necessarily comes with higher ideological risk than being an electrician or working for a heating and air conditioning business. Evangelicals will need to think about their skills, aptitudes, conscience, and risk tolerance in deciding what career to pursue.

Am I suggesting that Christians avoid riskier work environments or withdraw from the Fortune 500 corporate environment and other elite social institutions? Not at all. I'm simply pointing out that in a negative world, we can no longer assume that being Christian brings with it positive benefits or even that those who control these institutions will be neutral toward our Christian faith and beliefs. As Jesus taught his disciples, we must count the cost. Those who pursue careers in these "riskier" fields should enter them knowing that a potential cost is involved and that they may need the support of others in the Christian community if and when they end up suffering for the sake of Christ.

It's similar with our family choices or where we choose to live. Marriage is certainly not risk free in an age of no-fault divorce, but it does provide the potential for one spouse to continue earning money if the other is fired or feels compelled to resign from a job over their Christian beliefs. And if the couple was already living well below their means, all the better.

Living in a lower-cost city or region can likewise reduce risk, as can living in a more conservative versus a more progressive state, city, or neighborhood. Living close to extended family can also be helpful by creating an additional support network.

Again, none of this is to suggest that some professions or locations are off-limits to evangelicals. Some will decide they're well suited to working in finance in New York City or technology in Silicon Valley. Others will choose a different path, and no choice is entirely risk free. As I said earlier, there's no simple playbook or business plan for living in the negative world. But it is different from the past. Evangelical Christians need to consider their vocation and location to a greater extent than was necessary in the positive and neutral worlds.

A SPECIAL NOTE FOR PASTORS

Pastors may need to pay particular attention to the way they structure their lives. The pastor's job has never been easy, but the advent of the negative world has taken the stresses of pastoral life to a new level. Many pastors feel like they're in a pressure cooker environment with challenges facing them no matter what they do.

We see evidence of this in the increasing stress levels reported in surveys on pastoral burnout. In November 2021 the religious polling organization Barna Group released survey results showing that almost 40 percent of pastors had thought about leaving the ministry in the past year.[25] The number of people thinking of leaving the ministry increased by nine percentage points in less than a year, with younger pastors more likely to consider leaving than their older brethren. A quarter of pastors rated themselves as "unhealthy" in terms of well-being. David Kinnaman, CEO of Barna, noted that pastoral burnout was a rising concern even before COVID-19, suggesting that the end of the pandemic would not resolve these problems.[26]

Pastors aren't just talking about quitting, they *are* quitting. The *Washington Post* described an exodus of clergy in the pandemic year.[27] Even high-profile pastors have stepped down from their pulpits, such as Jason Meyer, successor of John Piper at Bethlehem Baptist Church in Minneapolis,[28] and Abraham Cho at Redeemer Presbyterian Church East Side in New York City.[29] Their jobs would typically have been considered pastoral dream jobs, serving at two of the most prestigious evangelical churches in the country. Yet these men stepped down voluntarily, without any personal moral scandals or improprieties.

The negative world comes with pressure from outside the church, such as the very real risk of coming under attack for merely preaching what the Bible teaches. But the growing culture war within evangelicalism is also adding to the pressure. Teachings on many issues, especially race relations and sexuality, are causing divisions in churches just as they are in schools and other institutions. Both Meyer and Cho resigned as they were experiencing pressure and controversy in their ministries on the topic of race. But other matters, such as whether to hold in-person services or to require masks, likewise became divisive during the COVID-19 pandemic.

Anything can become a "political" dispute today, and this makes it almost impossible for a pastor to avoid controversy and pressure from angry members in their congregation. If pastors require masks, some people will protest. If they don't require them, different people will. Consider what happened to David Platt, senior pastor of McLean Bible Church in Northern Virginia. When President Trump made a surprise appearance at his church one Sunday morning and requested prayer, Platt prayed for him. Then even though praying for political leaders is a direct biblical command, Platt was attacked for this.[30] Later, he was accused of the opposite problem, of being too woke, and his church was also sued over its internal election procedures.[31] The point isn't that "both sides" are wrong in these disputes or that pastors are right, but that it's now impossible in a negative world environment for pastors to avoid high-pressure and often high-stakes conflict situations. The negative world is fertile ground for disagreement and dissension to flourish in a divided American church.

Like all of us, pastors need to realize that living in a negative world will necessarily lead to more pressure on followers of Jesus, including those who shepherd them. This will require greater mental and emotional toughness. We see this clearly in the ministry of the apostle Paul in the midst of his own persecution. In one of his letters to the Corinthians, he recounts the various physical trials he was forced to endure, ranging from flogging to being shipwrecked to being stoned and left for dead. But he also details the mental and emotional strain he faced: "Besides everything else, I face daily the pressure of my concern for all the churches. Who is weak, and I do not feel weak? Who is led into sin, and I do not inwardly burn?" (2 Corinthians 11:28–29).

Though Paul faces this pressure and concern, he soldiers on through it all. We see this on display again in 2 Timothy, where even though he's been imprisoned as a common criminal, is facing execution, and has been deserted by his friends, he continues his mission. He preaches the gospel at his trial, writes a letter of exhortation to Timothy, and models through his own behavior the instructions he gives to his younger protégé.

While American pastors today may not be called to endure the physical trials Paul suffered, tougher mental and emotional trials are already a reality for many of them. Going forward, especially those who enter vocational ministry will need to count the cost, as they're likely to need greater mental and emotional resiliency, and prepare to face higher levels of conflict and stress than those faced by previous generations. There are likely many lessons to be learned, not only from the suffering of the early church but from brothers and sisters throughout history and around the world who have endured conflict in the past.

Practically, pastors will need to take active steps to mitigate or manage their stress. While this can be addressed in many ways, one example is to intentionally cultivate strong relationships with peers and mentors and staying close with them.[32] In the years to come, this will be more important than ever, as will good relationships with their elders and lay church leaders (or other similar roles, depending on denominational governance structures).

Another practical suggestion is for pastors to look for ways to reduce non-mission-related risks. Many pastors have sizable families and are poorly paid. Taking tough stands that might put their ministry job at risk can be doubly hard because of the financial stress they face. Operating under a bi-vocational model—adding a part-time, outside career—can help reduce that pressure and risk in some situations. (Lexington Theological Seminary conducted a study that found bi-vocational ministry "contributes to financial stability for both ministers and congregations.")[33]

For example, Presbyterian pastor C. R. Wiley, who has blue collar as well as pastoral skills, has acquired several rental properties over the years. He's said this brought him greater freedom of conscience. "In 2004 I found myself in a situation in which I had to choose between my pastorate and my conscience," he told me. "The doctrine of divine providence and the gift of persevering faith were there to help me, but it didn't hurt that I had eighteen tenants by then. That was important, because I also had a stay-at-home wife and three children under the age of ten."[34]

Not everybody can build a real estate portfolio, of course, but there are other options, such as retaining a part-time occupation (recall that the apostle Paul often worked as a tentmaker during his ministry). Or a person might consider entering the ministry later in life, after building marketplace skills and saving enough money to serve as a protective cushion against job loss. For people pursuing an aggressive savings strategy, one career option might be becoming a pastor as a second career.

The reality of higher stress and conflict for those called to pastorally minister the gospel in the negative world is here to stay. And while I've attempted to provide some practical suggestions and examples in this chapter, the overarching point is to develop resilience to mitigate the increased risk of life in the negative world. And that starts by understanding that times have changed. Each person who pursues a call to pastoral ministry will need to find a path to finding the mental and emotional resiliency to stand fast in the midst of the pressures sure to come.

Whether we're called to pastor or, like every Christian, called to follow Christ where we are, each of us must be thinking about how to structure our household life, counting the cost and exercising our God-given wisdom to become more resilient in the riskier environment of the negative world.

PART THREE

LEADING

INSTITUTIONALLY

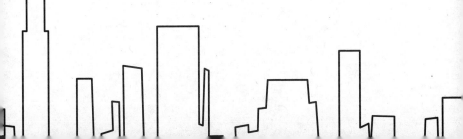

CHAPTER 7

PURSUE
INSTITUTIONAL
INTEGRITY

IT'S NO SECRET THAT IN CONTEMPORARY AMERICA, there's been a general decline of trust in institutions. Gallup, one of the key organizations that measures institutional trust, found that general trust levels in institutions fell to an all-time low in 2022. They found that Congress has an especially low approval score, having fallen to 7 percent. But Gallup's approval scores for "the church or organized religion" have also fallen to a three-decade low, to 31 percent and down six percentage points year over year.[1] That's better than most institutions, including public schools, newspapers, and large technology companies, but it's nothing to feel good about.

Declining trust in the church is likely linked to the period of decline in the status of Christianity since 1964. But it might also be the case that the church is facing the same challenges every institution is facing today. These survey results are certainly consistent with the declines seen in other institutions.

And it's hard to argue with these scores. Our institutions have not been performing well. We've been in a period of slow economic growth since the year 2000. The housing crash recession was so bad that it earned the nickname the "Great Recession." As of 2021, the Taliban are back in charge in Afghanistan. In 2022 high inflation made a comeback for the first time in forty years. Life expectancy is declining. There's extreme partisan polarization in the country. Problems like crime and homelessness are trending up in our cities. Many institutions have become infected by ideologies that compromise their ability to deliver on their core mission.

Along with many of our social institutions, evangelical churches have not always proven worthy of trust. This only weakens them as they come under the more intense pressure of the negative world. Those who seek a position as a leader or currently have leadership positions in such institutions—churches, parachurch ministries, or even organizations like businesses owned by evangelicals—need to prioritize institutional integrity. I use the word *integrity* here not just in the sense of a greater culture of honesty and ethical behavior, but also in the sense of structural integrity. Like a bridge or building, or a ship or an airplane, evangelical institutions must be able to retain their shape when the pressures of the negative world bear down on them hard.

Both evangelical and evangelical-run institutions will need to create and sustain this institutional integrity across three dimensions: trustworthiness, competence, and missional focus. Additionally, their leaders need to have a long-term intergenerational perspective on their institutions' well-being.

TRUSTWORTHINESS AND COMPETENCE

When a friend took over as board chair of an evangelical organization in 2020, he listed as one of his goals for the board, "Be a trustworthy institution with funds, families." He understood that in a world of declining trust it was important for his organization to intentionally focus on building and maintaining trust. In the past, people may have had an implicit or assumed trust with institutions, especially the evangelical church or a nonprofit Christian organization. But that is no longer the case. Rather than assuming trust as a default from their constituency, this leader knew he had to actively earn and steward trust.

While trustworthiness can be a broad term, I'm using it here to refer to baseline morals and ethics. This would include the personal moral behavior of the leaders and employees of institutions—being above reproach, for example (1 Timothy 3:2). It can also mean appropriately managing institutional funds and operations. These aspects of trustworthiness should be a simple baseline element of institutional leadership, but alas, that is not always the case today.

Many churches and other Christian institutions have a variety of moral, ethical, operational, and even criminal problems. Abuse scandals in the Catholic Church have grabbed most of the negative headlines, but evangelicals have suffered quite a few of their own.[2] Pastors, such as Carl Lentz of Hillsong New York City, are far too regularly caught in extramarital affairs, sometimes multiple affairs.[3] A number of prominent churches continue to be run without any checks and balances, a recipe for things to go wrong—and they often do.

Christian institutions sometimes compound this by trying to hide their malfeasance and silence whistleblowers. Former college professor Stephen Baskerville wrote a report for the James G. Martin Center for Academic Renewal about how Christian colleges abuse non-disparagement agreements and mandatory arbitration clauses to silence dissenters and would-be whistleblowers.[4] When church scandals erupt, it isn't surprising to find that those churches have been using tactics like these to keep problems from coming to light.[5] Professors and ministry staff are often poorly paid and have big families to provide for, so they're often in no position to blow the whistle on malfeasance, saying no when their institutions demand silence in return for severance pay.

A lot of ministries have also grotesquely enriched the people who run them, such as the infamous case of Kenneth Copeland and his multiple private jets.[6] But even those who aren't identified with the prosperity gospel can also earn eyebrow-raising sums from their ministries. For example, alleged financial mismanagement and compensation problems were at least partially behind the fall of James MacDonald, former pastor of Harvest Bible Chapel, a Chicago-area megachurch.[7]

There's nothing inherently wrong with being rich, but there are legitimate ways for people to acquire wealth that don't require paying themselves a lot of money from their nonprofit ministries. Going into ministry shouldn't require a vow of poverty, and pastors should be well compensated for their work where possible, but their paychecks and benefits should not cause anyone to do a double take. Churches and religious organizations need to be even more rigorous in operating aboveboard and with transparency in the negative world.

At the same time, we should not be surprised when people, especially those empowered to lead organizations, stumble in some way. People and all human institutions are flawed by sin. We can't earn trustworthiness by being perfect any more than we could earn our salvation that way. Perfection is an impossible standard. But what we can do, knowing that a level of moral failure is inevitable at some point for every person and institution, is practice repentance in our personal failings and take appropriate, responsible action when there are organizational problems.

Trustworthiness doesn't always equate to being liked by the world outside the church. People who dislike or even hate what the Bible teaches are unlikely to put much trust in those who hold to its truths—no matter what we do. Being trustworthy is not about pleasing everyone or an obsession with public popularity. If evangelical institutions are unpopular, it should be for the right reasons, not because of their own institutional failures or the sins of their leaders.

In other words, if we're working for an institution, we need to focus on operating in a trustworthy manner. Far too many evangelical institutions have fallen short and need to rebuild trust with the public—and even with their own constituency. Additionally, we need to ensure that our institutions and their leaders are competent. There's just no substitute for institutional competence and operational excellence, yet we live in a world where that's too often lacking. Especially in the higher-pressure environment of the negative world, competence is a must.

MISSIONAL FOCUS

Every organization has a mission it was founded to pursue. Churches seek to make disciples and equip their flock for the work of ministry. Food banks, homelessness ministries, missionary-support organizations, and college ministries all have a mission they're trying to achieve for the glory of God. A Christian-owned business also has a mission it's trying to achieve in the pursuit of earning an honest profit. Every institution needs to have a clear sense of its mission and to remain focused on delivering that mission in the face of distractions and pressure to change.

The cold reality is that outside actors frequently target

institutions who have a mission they don't like, trying to force it to change course. Some denominations, for example, have secret or semi-secret factions seeking to exert influence over their direction.[8] In the most extreme cases, these activists capture control of the institution and reorient it away from the original mission toward their own priorities. For example, this befell most of the mainline denominations, which were successfully steered away from a gospel-centered mission toward one centered around secular-driven progressive social policies and liberal theology.[9]

Many people, and some powerful secular entities, don't want institutions to be mission focused. This is even the case in the corporate world, where one would ordinarily expect profitability and other such goals to predominate. We can see this in the case of the company Coinbase. CEO Brian Armstrong, concerned about how social issues and politics had started to consume his company's focus, explicitly stated that Coinbase would henceforth be "a mission focused company," with more effort on areas like building great products and without employee activism for social and political issues on the job.[10] This caused significant controversy, with the company offering severance packages to those who wanted to voluntarily leave because they didn't agree with the new direction. Over sixty employees took the offer, about 5 percent of the employee base.[11]

Within two months, the *New York Times* published critical pieces about the company, starting with an article accusing Coinbase of racism.[12] Someone then leaked the company's payroll data to the *Times*, which ran multiple articles accusing it of underpaying minorities in an analysis that made no adjustments for education or experience levels.[13] It's likely these articles would not have appeared but for Coinbase's decision to prohibit activism on the job. Similar problems hit the software company Basecamp after it announced it would no longer allow discussion of social and political issues on the company's internal chat boards.[14] A third of that company's employees quit.

This pressure on corporations comes not just from activist employees and the media but also increasingly from investment funds. The so-called Environmental Social and Governance (ESG) goals movement is attempting to shift business toward political priorities in these areas, such as climate change, or diversity, equity, and inclusion. Major institutional money managers like Black Rock, which have large shareholdings in many corporations, are strong promoters of ESG.[15]

Any significantly sized organization in America that wishes to focus on its mission and not promote secular progressive ideologies can be expected to be subjected to intense pressure, both internal and external, to reorient itself away from mission toward these political objectives. This includes even evangelical churches, schools, and ministries.

Obviously, because circumstances change, organizations need to adapt and adjust their missional focus over time. A church needs to think about how it serves its neighborhood needs to change as the neighborhood changes, such as by adjusting to demographic shifts. But evangelicalism, whose strength comes from its adaptability, is always at risk of chasing fads and being blown here and there by the wind.

The biggest threat to missional integrity for religious organizations today, as it was with Coinbase, is linking its religious mission with political or social activism. Undoubtedly—and this was especially true with the culture war churches of the positive world—there was a tight linkage between evangelicalism and conservative politics. And though only a small minority, some churches did promote pro-Trump political rallies during their services.[16] This combination is clearly wrong.

We also see this happening with the rise of woke politics within evangelical churches, particularly on the topic of race. This woke turn in the evangelical church took place not long after the secular "Great Awokening" circa 2014. Race relations is certainly an appropriate topic for preaching, and there's sadly a great deal of room for improvement on racial matters in America. Many ministries and figures have long had some type of racial justice or reconciliation as part of their mission. The long and admirable career of John Perkins is a great example of this. Jonathan Wilson-Hartgrove's Rutba House intentional community in Durham, North Carolina, is another.

But what's notable about today's evangelical woke turn is the lack of provenance of the focus on race in many of these churches and the fact that many of them have little direct tie to blacks or other minority groups, such as by being located in or near a historically or emerging black neighborhood. This shift, coming in the wake of a similar secular shift and adopting language similar to secular, non-Christian movements, raises legitimate questions about the extent to which this woke turn is truly theological or missionally driven versus simply embracing yet another secular social trend.

Whether the problem is conservative politics linked with the mission of the church, Trumpism, wokeness, or some other matter, every evangelical church and evangelical-related institution needs to review its mission, make sure it is clear and aligned with its identity and purpose, and then seek to remain focused on that mission.

Some institutions may have a mission that includes specific focus areas in our world, including political activism. Or it might be an evangelical-owned business, a ministry or nonprofit focused on the environment, a ministry focused on some aspect of racial justice, or a church that wants to reach many different parts of a multicultural neighborhood. In these cases, that specific focus area is integral to the mission. In other cases, however, pressure from the outside world or activists from inside or outside the church or organization seeks to refocus the organization away from its mission toward their own political or social objectives.

The lesson of the mainline denominations serves as a powerful object lesson for the danger of giving in to those pressures and how that road leads to institutional and missional death.[17]

INSTITUTIONAL INTEGRITY TODAY—AND TOMORROW

Another aspect of institutional integrity is also important to keep in mind—the inter-generational component.

In significant ways, our legacy is not what we do when we're on the public stage but what happens after we leave it. It's not just about how successful a church is while a particular pastor is leading it but what happens on his successor's watch. Leaders may not have full authority in selecting a successor or be able to fully control what happens after they're gone, but they certainly have some role in and responsibility for it. That's true for corporate CEOs, and it's true for Christian leaders too.

The builders of the great cathedrals in the world started work they knew couldn't be completed in their own lifetimes, taking a multigenerational perspective. This is commendable and something leaders in our time would do well to consider. Sadly, some leaders today adopt the perspective of King Hezekiah of Judah, who took the opposite view, as we see in this famous passage, 2 Kings 20:16–19:

> Isaiah said to Hezekiah, "Hear the word of the LORD: The time will surely come when everything in your palace, and

all that your predecessors have stored up until this day, will be carried off to Babylon. Nothing will be left, says the LORD. And some of your descendants, your own flesh and blood who will be born to you, will be taken away, and they will become eunuchs in the palace of the king of Babylon."

"The word of the LORD you have spoken is good," Hezekiah replied. For he thought, "Will there not be peace and security in my lifetime?"

Peace and security in his own lifetime trumped Hezekiah's concern even for his own flesh-and-blood descendants.

The Bible often speaks about our *ways*, about the path we're on in life. One way leads to life, and another one leads to death. The same is true for institutions. If an institution meets a bad fate after its leader leaves, that leader may have been complicit in sending it down the path to that destination. If our church or organization goes off the rails after we leave or pass on, then we likely deserve a share in the blame for that.

One solution to this problem is to encourage more of an intergenerational view as we lead our institutions, intentionally stewarding them for long-term integrity. How to do that isn't always obvious, but merely thinking about the question can often add new perspectives to present decisions. For example, building a church around a single celebrity pastor can lead to challenges when there's a leadership transition.

Churches and other institutions need to carry out succession planning, contingency planning, long-term forecasting. and other tasks necessary for longer-term risk management. They need to address problems forthrightly rather than deferring them into the future. They need to avoid accumulated unfunded liabilities such as deferred building maintenance. The decisions institutional leaders make should be made with long-term as well as near-term considerations.

While pursuing theological orthodoxy and missional effectiveness, we should consider how few churches stay effective for more than a generation or so. One of the justifications given for the evangelical focus on church planting is that newer churches draw most of their members from the unchurched while older churches draw primarily from those who have been attending church elsewhere.[18] This is an implicit acknowledgment that missional effectiveness falls off quickly with age. Our cities and towns have many architecturally significant church buildings, many of which have closed or are in decline, showing that churches don't necessarily last forever.[19]

Some mainline churches have significant, strategically located real estate assets and endowments, to say nothing of their inherited institutional and brand capital. One example, albeit an extreme one, is Trinity Church Wall Street, an Episcopal parish in the heart of New York's financial district with an endowment of $6 billion.[20] Many of these assets were built up by faithful believers of years past. Some are still stewarded well, but others have now fallen under the control of those who no longer hold to traditional Christian beliefs. Ensuring that doesn't happen in institutions we're responsible for is part of our stewardship mandate.

Evangelical churches are vibrant today, but will they still be vibrant fifty or a hundred years from now? This is a question for church leaders to ponder. Other evangelical institutions like Christian colleges and seminaries face a more near-term reckoning as enrollments decline and negative world pressures increase.[21] Evangelical leaders can't consider the long-term success or even survival of their institutions a given. They have to be an explicit focus.

In a world where trust in institutions is in deep decline and there are enormous negative world pressures to capitulate on traditional Christian doctrine or otherwise align with secular ideologies on various matters, evangelical institutions need to develop institutional integrity. This means asking what it means to be a trustworthy institution when many institutions aren't. It means being competent in a world hungry for excellence. And it means staying focused on mission amid the pressure to drift away—and sustaining that mission successfully across generations.

CHAPTER 8

PURSUE COMMUNITY STRENGTH

DOMINANT MAJORITY GROUPS SELDOM HAVE TO worry too much about how to culturally and institutionally sustain their community. That's because the mainstream institutions of society are designed in a manner consistent with and even reinforces their values.

Consider public schools. When there was a large Protestant majority in America, these schools reinforced Christian morality.[1] They also inculcated traditional American values like fair play and sportsmanship. They even had public prayer until the Supreme Court outlawed it in 1962.[2] Today, however, they attempt to inculcate values in children that conflict with Christianity. Some of them consciously attempt to subvert parental authority as well.[3]

Or think about the Boy Scouts' emergence from the Protestant muscular Christianity movement and their members' oath: "On my honor I will do my best to do my duty to God and my country."[4] Churches played a key role in the spread of scouting, and even now some churches still sponsor scout troops.[5] Yet now the Boy Scouts have drifted far from their traditional mission. They aren't even the Boy Scouts anymore, having admitted girls and renamed their flagship program Scouts BSA after a series of major sexual abuse scandals.[6]

America's earliest and most prestigious colleges were also explicitly Protestant Christian in nature, established to train ministers.[7] Even into the mid-twentieth century, they still embodied many of those values as they then existed among the liberal Protestant WASP establishment. Today, Harvard's chief chaplain is an avowed atheist.[8]

Up through the 1950s, the major institutions of American society—government, the military, universities, business—were interlinked culturally and institutionally with elite American Protestantism. Hence there was almost no conflict between being a Christian, of a white Protestant variety at any rate, and being a business executive, government official, or non-profit leader. Those institutions were not only positive toward Christianity, but they actively embedded the values and preferences of the American Protestant majority. To be sure, some of these were cultural and not merely religious, but clearly some religious values were included.

LIFE AS A MINORITY GROUP

The experience of minority groups is generally very different, however. Because the mainstream institutions and culture of society aren't designed with their values, and may frequently be contrary to their values, they have to self-consciously focus on sustaining their culture and community life. This includes creating their own institutions to serve their community specifically and creating unique practices that demarcate and sustain community life. They have to specifically steward their own community well-being and mobilize to advocate and act on its behalf.

None of this necessarily indicates that the minority group in question is hostile to mainstream society. But even where they are positive toward it, they understand that they need to sustain their own community, values, and traditions.

The need to steward the strength and well-being of their own community applies to racial, ethnic, and religious minorities. But the actual circumstances of each are different. Racial minorities are visibly distinct, and people can't change their race or ethnicity. Religion is different. In some cases, it functions similar to ethnicity. This is the case with Judaism, a religion primarily made up of those of Jewish descent—a people group. In other cases, religion is not ethnically bound. Christianity in America is like that. This makes Christians as a religious minority different from racial or ethnic minorities.

One important difference is that Christians can abandon their faith and no longer be considered a Christian, whereas racial and ethnic minorities can't escape being treated as members of their group. Some critics of my three worlds model have pointed to the experience of black Christians in the 1950s as an example of why this wasn't really a positive world for Christianity.[9] But it's obvious that they were suffering discrimination for being black, not for being Christian. The discrimination would not have ended if they had renounced their faith.

Again, I would stress that just because Christianity was softly institutionalized in the 1950s does not mean America was run in accordance with Christian values or without injustice then. Additionally, visibly distinct minorities are also always immediately recognized as such, whereas it's ordinarily not immediately obvious whether someone is Christian.[10] A black Christian will immediately be seen as black but not necessarily Christian.[11]

As I've mentioned before, Christians as a whole are no longer a dominant majority in America.[12] They're now a minority, at least in the most powerful institutions and domains of society. Many Christian moral values have been de facto evicted from major social institutions. Evangelicals especially hold few top positions in important institutions. This status as a minority is less consequential than being a racial or ethnic minority, but it still has consequences. It's also a relatively new and thus uncomfortable situation for American Protestants, especially white Protestants who don't have any other experience as a minority to draw on.

In today's world, evangelicals aren't a majority, either by themselves or as part of a larger Christian group. We don't run society's major institutions, and sometimes we barely have a seat at the table in them. Our core values are now in disfavor. In a negative world, where the institutions of culture see Christian identity and beliefs as negative status markers, the old model of thinking and acting like a majority needs to be jettisoned. Evangelicals need to learn to act like a minority and spend more time and effort focused on sustaining their own communities and beliefs.

This is why I've said evangelicals need to have a shift in emphasis toward becoming more of a counterculture. Minorities must operate at some level as strong countercultures or subcultures in order to sustain themselves. This is the shift evangelicals need to make.

This doesn't mean evangelicals should abandon mission and evangelism or become hostile or hateful toward other groups. They should not resign themselves to doing nothing or no longer caring about the country or the general welfare of society. But it does them no good to focus on these things if they don't also tend to the strength and well-being of their own evangelical communities, much the same way other minority groups have had to tend to theirs. We can't give somebody something we don't have ourselves. Strengthening our communities will enable evangelicals to have a genuinely Christian place they can invite others into, and this can serve as a base from which to pursue outward mission. This kind of well-formed, embodied identity is more important than ever in the negative world.[13]

Relatedly, evangelicals no longer need to view themselves as bearing the same level of responsibility for mainstream institutions as they did in the past. Evangelicals are no longer in charge of those institutions today, and the people who are in charge are often promoting things directly contrary to Christian beliefs and American traditions. If an evangelical senses an opportunity to make a positive change in an institution, they should take advantage of it. But utilizing an opportunity is different from pursuing a priority.

In the negative world, then, it's legitimate for evangelicals to rethink their relationship with mainstream institutions, adopting a less transformational approach with less investment in them. Some of these shifts are already happening organically as Christians recognize that the culture is no longer accepting of their Christian beliefs and perspectives.

LEARNING FROM MINORITIES
WHO HAVE GONE BEFORE

Again, there is no map or ready-made strategic plan to tell evangelicals how to strengthen and sustain their community in the negative world. This is uncharted territory for people used to being a majority, or at least part of the majority group. Evangelicals can certainly seek to learn from other religious minorities who have experience as minorities in a culture opposed to their values as they develop approaches for this. But a number of factors set the case of today's American evangelicals apart from other groups.

For one thing, though no longer a majority, evangelicals remain a significantly large bloc of people. This makes them unlike, say, Jews or Sikhs who are numerically very small minorities in the United States.[14] Lessons can still be drawn from studying smaller minority groups, but the application may be limited however impressive those communities might be in retaining a unique identity within a majority culture.

In addition, evangelicals in America—like Christians generally—are themselves highly diverse. We have denominational divisions and theological divisions on topics like baptism. And there's significant racial diversity within evangelicalism, even if not all who fall into the evangelical category still want to call themselves evangelical. For evangelicals who are racial minorities, race rather than religion may be more salient to their thinking. Other minority groups likewise have internal divisions frequently not visible or thought about by outsiders.[15] They sometimes operate separately, other times together. We should expect the same among American evangelicals, except that given their aggregate size, many of evangelicalism's subcommunities probably have the necessary scale to operate relatively on their own.

The situation today is also different from the past in that there is no clear majority group to replace the older WASP establishment culture. A professional-managerial class that is not ethnic or religious but ideological and economic in character dominates elite society today.[16] This is in essence a minority group that controls the country, one capable of co-opting the most able members of other groups. Additionally, America is a post-Christian nation, which creates something of an allergic reaction to anything particularly Christian in its institutions.

As some have noted, this makes it different from a country that was never Christian to begin with.[17]

With those considerations in mind, where should evangelicals look for models? One model worth consideration is early- to mid-twentieth-century Catholicism. As with evangelicals today, Catholics were at that time a sizable, diverse minority. Yet their Christianity was disfavored, and they sometimes faced overt discrimination from the Protestant majority. They had to develop ways to sustain their communities and beliefs in this environment as well as take on other functions, like assisting new immigrants in adapting to America.

Granted, the ethnic nature of these communities also bound them together in ways mere Catholicism may not have. Catholicism has long been more ethnically partitioned than some would like to admit.[18] This was especially true where there were language barriers between Catholic immigrant communities. Yet we also see that Catholics came together at times, as they did to support the Irish Catholic John F. Kennedy in his run for president.

Catholics built their own churches, their own schools, and their own universities. They held catechism classes for their youth and created their own social organizations like the Knights of Columbus. They long held to uniquely Catholic practices like abstaining from eating meat on Fridays, traditional practices that set them apart from the rest of the country. They had distinct visible symbols like rosaries and crucifixes. They became very patriotic, even exaggeratedly so at times, to show that they were authentically American too.[19]

The role of Catholic universities is of particular of interest. Today, most originally Protestant colleges have only a vestigial connection to their faith or denomination, if that.[20] Those that have a strong religious dimension, like most evangelical "Christian colleges," are chosen primarily on account of their religious content, not the academic. While Catholic colleges like Notre Dame may not adhere to Catholic orthodoxy in many respects, they still operate both as real mainstream universities and as ones where the Catholic identity remains central.

These institutions have provided a home base for many identifiably Catholic intellectuals, giving them national prominence few Protestants can muster. This includes people like now Supreme Court Justice Amy Coney Barrett, political scientist Patrick Deneen, and architect Duncan Stroik.

By contrast, Protestants relied on mainstream institutions (like the Ivy League) to be the home and breeding ground for their top intellectuals. As the establishment and mainline denominations collapsed, Protestantism was evicted from those institutions, and this has left a void yet to be filled.

The Mormons are another good example to consider. Their religion, seen as a heretical sect from the position of mainstream Christianity, had to sustain itself independently. After a long period of persecution, the Mormons in some ways became even more American than the average Protestant American. One reason Utah is such a successful state today is that it still embodies these "retro Protestant" values of hard work, thrift, marriage, children, and community.[21] The Mormons embraced mainstream institutions like the public schools[22] and Boy Scouts while maintaining their own sectarian ones to sustain their faith.

But as the nation has shifted, the Mormons have also been shifting, perhaps in ways evangelicals might judge good or bad depending on their perspective. The Mormons are withdrawing from the Boy Scouts in order to create their own youth organization, for example. One reason is the globalization of Mormonism and the need to provide a common global experience. But it's clear that they also don't like the direction the Boy Scouts are heading.[23] It will be informative to watch the

Mormons in coming years to observe how they navigate these cultural shifts.

FOCUS AREAS FOR STRENGTHENING EVANGELICAL COMMUNITIES

If evangelicals in a negative world must necessarily shift toward a more passive engagement with cultural institutions and develop their own inwardly focused, community-strengthening initiatives, what might that look like? And where to focus? Four areas of potential focus are education; equipping, not insulating; embracing counter-catechesis; and repairing our own sexual economy.

EDUCATION

Education is an area where evangelicals have already begun to restructure their approach, and so it provides helpful clues and lessons to guide us in thinking through what needs to be done more broadly.

In the past two decades, there's been an explosion of evangelical Christian schools of various types,[24] as well as significant growth in homeschooling.[25] Evangelicals have recognized that the public education system has not only deteriorated in its ability to educate kids well but increasingly no longer reflects traditionally Christian values and is often at odds with them. Unsurprisingly, evangelicals have been exiting that system year after year.[26] Of course, many evangelicals still send their children to public schools and will continue to do so in the future, but growing numbers have been leaving them, voting with their feet.

This exit from public schools by evangelicals has been controversial. Some argue that it's motivated by hostility toward public education.[27] Others worry that leaving hurts poor or minority children, and there is some truth to this. Undoubtedly, poorly performing public schools are harming many children's futures, and the withdrawal of evangelicals and others from those schools hurts those institutions in several ways. But evangelicals are under no obligation to send their kids to poorly performing schools that also actively seek to undermine their beliefs, and they shouldn't feel guilty when they decide to leave.

The reality is that evangelicals don't run the public schools, and evangelical Christian beliefs are now treated as illegitimate or harmful in many of them. This means evangelicals aren't responsible for the outcomes of these schools and should not feel obligated to remain invested in them or send their children to them. Many evangelical parents, however, will judge that the public schools are the best option for their children. This is a legitimate choice.

The point is not that evangelical parents should never send their kids to public schools or never be involved with public schools, but that they should consider themselves free to make what they believe to be the best choice for their children without feeling obligated to the public school system. When Roman Catholic communities believed that the public schools were too Protestant for their convictions, they established a large Catholic school network to educate their children.[28] This is how minority groups act. Similarly, now that evangelicals are a de facto minority group, and public schools are sometimes often overtly anti-Christian in their teachings, similar logic applies for us.

Back to the Protestant-dominated America of the 1950s, one could argue that Protestants, including evangelicals, had a direct responsibility for the public schools institutionally. They were influential in their creation and adoption as an American cultural institution. But today, as a minority that's no longer in charge, that's no longer the case. Again, I want to be clear that I'm not advocating a wholesale abandonment of the public school system. If an evangelical is in a position to improve public schools, that should be done. But not many are in that position, and the number is decreasing each year. Realistically, today even evangelical superintendents or principals have limited power to make changes on account of a thicket of constraining rules, laws, and judicial rulings.

Being a minority that's no longer in charge means that the mainstream institutions of society are now the responsibility of the people who are actually in charge and leading them. The problems we see today in the public schools and other institutions of American culture are a reflection of the ideas, convictions, and capabilities of those in charge. And unfortunately, the values of those running these institutions are often opposed to Christianity, and their general competence level is low.[29]

I stress this point because recognizing this reality necessitates making a psychological shift. Majorities naturally think about how to transform, influence, and shape the key organizations and institutions of society because they're used to being in charge of them or identifying with them at some level. But minorities, who almost by definition aren't in charge and who may not identify strongly with those institutions, must think differently. As American Protestants recognize the shift from dominant majority to unpopular minority, they must make this shift from majority to minority mindset. This won't be easy—or popular. It will result in a lot of criticism and attempts to delegitimize evangelical attempts to develop alternatives to the public school model.

It should not be surprising that rhetoric around the "common good" has come to the fore as evangelicals have started organically adjusting to a minority position.[30] Functionally,

however, the idea of the common good works to keep evangelicals invested in the mainstream systems and not tend to our
own community specifically. If we start acting like the minority we are, this will surely draw hostility, perhaps even from
within the church. We should never let other people's hostility
drive us to respond with hate, but we must also have the forti-
tude to chart the course that's right even if it draws criticism.

In summary, being a cultural minority, as evangelicals are
in the negative world, means thinking and acting like a minority, and this may require declining to take responsibility for
struggling cultural institutions and developing alternate ones
of our own.

EQUIPPING, NOT INSULATING

While some evangelicals sought to lead and even transform
social institutions, others in evangelical culture and education
adopted another strategy. One that was more of a countercultural approach oriented around avoiding negative influence
from the surrounding society. It was a strategy of insulation.
For example, parents of homeschooled children, including even
non-evangelical homeschoolers, have been known to boast
about how their children are ignorant of the basics of popular
culture.[31] Evangelical parents have also been known for prohibiting their children from listening to secular pop music.[32]

The neutral world environment in which this emerged was
ideal for a strategy of insulation. This was the era in which
the great mass market common culture of the midcentury era
was fragmenting.[33] We went from three TV networks to "57
channels and nothing on"[34] to bespoke media for each person. In a fragmented, pluralistic culture, people could hope
to curate a cultural environment for themselves to suit their
preferences. Most of the major institutions like corporations
remained essentially culturally and politically neutral.

Today, there's no escape from secular culture and ideologies. Every institution and every subculture is under immense pressure to actively promote them. This is even true of traditional escapist leisure activities like watching the NFL, which now boasts that "football is gay,"[35] or video games.[36] Every corporation of any size also expects its employees to actively support these various ideologies.[37]

In the negative world, where the culture is explicitly negative toward Christianity and its beliefs, a strategy of insulation is no longer possible. Parents, pastors, and others must be actively equipping people to understand and live in this new, more challenging environment in which there is no escape from the pressure.

This means that providing your children with a traditional or classical Christian education is not enough. They also need to be educated about today's culture and how to navigate it. As an example, they need to be trained in how to understand modern media so they can avoid being taken in by "fake news" and conspiracy theories, as well as how to avoid falling prey to the major media's ability to create the illusion of public consensus on topics.[38] And while restricting access to technology can be appropriate for some age groups, at some point children need to be equipped to responsibly use smartphones and social media. As adults they will be on at least some social media platforms.

Children today need to be equipped and built up in an explicitly Christian faith—discipled to follow Jesus in a culture opposed to him—in ways that actively equip them for the challenges they'll experience in modern American society.

COUNTER-CATECHESIS

Counter-catechesis is related to or an extension of equipping. Growing up in a rural fundamentalist church, there was a lot I didn't learn. I didn't know what the Nicene Creed was, for example. But I did learn all about the Bible in Sunday school and church services. By the time I graduated high school, I knew it cold. Today, it's no secret that many children, after eighteen years of growing up in an evangelical church, can't tell you what a Christian is supposed to believe. Instead, they believe in the vague spirituality of Moralistic Therapeutic Deism,[39] with little substantive knowledge of the Bible or theology.

Something is wrong in how we're teaching the Bible, and we must do a better job to ensure that both children and adults know the basics of God's Word and what Christians believe.

That said, we can't assume that simply teaching people the Bible or Christian theology is the answer to this problem. Explicit counter-catechesis is also needed to equip people to navigate the negative world. It's not enough to teach them what to believe; we must also teach them what not to believe. This is consistent with some historic church confessions, which, in addition to affirming what they held to be true, also explicitly listed what they held to be false.[40] Children and adult Christians need to be taught what society at large unbiblically believes and why we, as Christians, don't believe those things.

Again, minorities have long had to do this. For example, Jews in America have to explain what Christmas is and why they don't celebrate it to their children. And in the negative world, Christians have to do similar things. This will of necessity focus on areas where society's ideologies and practices are in conflict with Christianity.

REPAIRING OUR SEXUAL ECONOMY

Another major challenge affecting secular society is the dysfunction of its sexual economy. Falling marriage rates,[41] too high (if stable to declining) rates of divorce,[42] falling fertility rates that are now well below replacement levels,[43] a 40 percent out-of-wedlock birth rate,[44] rampant exposure to hard-core online pornography, and the normalization of casual sex[45] all attest to this.

Culture war evangelicals have tended to direct their anger about this outward, toward a secular society that has promoted many of these concerns. But it's well known that these trends affect the church as well. Whether or not its divorce rates are higher, lower, or the same as society as a whole can be debated, but there's no dispute that there's a lot of divorce in the evangelical world.[46] And there's no disputing that pornography consumption is a major problem for evangelicals.[47]

Part of the adjustment to minority status is our learning to focus less on the splinter in another's eye and focus on the beam stuck in our own, to borrow from the words of Jesus. This means evangelicals should try to refocus their criticism and energy away from transforming secular society, where the prospects for materially changing culture in the near-term are poor, toward first repairing our own sexual economy.

Again, this doesn't mean a complete abandonment of secular activism by any means, as there will always be those God calls to that role. But in the negative world, the evangelical church must first be focused on removing that log from of our own eye. We should seek to create a counterculture *in the church* that models God's intended created order and Christian teaching. As Paul said, "What business is it of mine to judge those outside the church? Are you not to judge those inside? God will judge those outside" (1 Corinthians 5:12–13). We must first live out God's ways in our own lives, families, and churches. Only then, and only by God's grace, will we have any future hope of bringing change to secular society.

One area of particular concern is the evangelical church's growing embrace of post-familialism. That is, as marriage rates have fallen in secular society and many areas of the country such as urban centers have become dominated by singles, evangelicals are starting to normalize and affirm long-term or permanent singleness as a valid status for the ordinary person.

A Google search for the "gift of singleness" returns a large number of hits—even when qualified with words like *God* and so finding only religious articles. Undoubtedly, you've heard or seen an evangelical pastor or thought leader use the phrase *gift of singleness*. As the pews are filled with more and more unhappy singles, the default pastoral response has often been to show how singleness is an authentic calling for Christians— even a superior one in some ways.

But there are problems with this approach. It essentially rationalizes our declining levels of family formation as theologically valid.

First, we must acknowledge that there are "those who choose to live like eunuchs for the sake of the kingdom of heaven" (Matthew 19:12). But singlehood has never been understood as an ordinary calling for large numbers of Christians. Marriage with children has always been the normal and ordinary pattern of life for the vast majority of people—not for everyone, but for most. If you're someone for whom it is not good to be alone, or being alone is painful for you, talk of the "gift of singleness" is cold comfort.

It's understandable that pastors want to lessen this pain somehow. Unfortunately, they're often ill-equipped for this and don't understand the realities many single people face. Most pastors are married, often married young, and typically have children.[48] Few of them have had much experience with dating in today's world, particularly not on behalf of older age groups where many singles now find themselves. Even their single congregants likely don't understand the full ramifications of long-term singleness.

For example, an academic research report found that for

a group of women studied, singles were more likely to suffer from depression and loneliness and even die sooner than women who married.[49] Someone who is single at age forty may already be unhappy, but consider that they on average have forty more years of life to go. What is it like to still be single at age fifty, sixty, or even seventy? While there have always been single people in our culture, today we're seeing growing numbers of adults as singles, and this has wider implications for society and the church.[50]

Clearly, some people face real challenges when it comes to marrying, especially for women. Women, many of whom prefer not to marry men with less educational attainment than they have, are now obtaining as much as 60 percent of all college degrees.[51] That creates challenges for both men and women, as does the traditional female skew of church attendance. These challenges should not be minimized.

While acknowledging the challenges singles face and providing resources to better incorporate them into the church community, evangelical leaders also need to work hard at promoting marriages among their people. The church must not sell out its members' futures by giving up on this emphasis, no matter how difficult or countercultural it might be.

A community that's heavily nonfamilial—where its members regularly watch porn, don't marry, enter into short-term sexual commitments, and experience frequent divorce—is a weak community. If the evangelical church wants to survive and thrive in the negative world, it can't be conformed to the world in this manner. And the place to start is not with attacks on the broader culture or knee-jerk condemnations of others, but by intentionally repairing our own sexual economy. As I discuss in chapter 10, a community with a healthy sexual economy can be an enabler of mission and evangelism in a negative world culture.

SUMMARY

A lot of evangelical thought about the nature of the church is rooted in an assumption of a Christian majority, Christian normative society in which the church is strong and its goal is to save those who happen to still be lost. For example, consider the early twentieth-century English theologian William Temple's quip that "the church is the only institution that exists for the sake of people who are not yet members." This is one you still hear repeated today. The Anglican Church in North America has a diocese called "A Church for the Sake of Others" that expresses similar sentiments.

But again, we can't give somebody something we don't have ourselves. If we don't have strong communities rooted in the faith once for all delivered to the saints, we have nothing to invite other people into. Having a robust identity as a unique community—and yes, as a minority group in a negative world—is a necessary precondition to effective and genuine evangelism and service to others.[52]

This is the approach we see in the New Testament, where the early church was a minority faith. They honored the government, but they did not view themselves as responsible for the institutions of the Roman imperium. They focused their efforts on teaching and discipling people into a countercultural identity, community, and way of life. And this was what set them apart from the larger culture where they lived and worked. Their focus wasn't on culture wars as we conceive of them today, but on developing their own cultural identity and strengthening their own community life.

Much of the New Testament was written specifically to address matters that were weakening the church, especially false teaching, disunity, and sexual licentiousness. To be clear, there was also a profound external mission of spreading the gospel, but the health of the church itself was given a high priority as well. As Paul once wrote, putting special emphasis on the church itself, "Let us do good to all people, especially to those who belong to the family of believers" (Galatians 6:10). As American Christians living in the negative world, we, too, must learn to be more intentional in developing a unique Christian identity and developing the strength of our own Christian community.

CHAPTER 9

PURSUE OWNERSHIP

WITH THE STATUS OF CHRISTIANITY DECLINING AFTER 1964, wherever evangelicals felt the country was heading in the wrong direction they built a parallel economy, giving particular focus to cultural products. We see the fruits of these efforts today in the numerous evangelical publishing houses and contemporary Christian music producers and radio stations.

Now as we transition to the negative world, evangelicals need to think even more broadly about ownership. An overreliance on mainstream institutions exposes Christians to increasing negative pressure and influence, making us fragile.[1] In the last chapter we looked at the area of primary and secondary education, where social trends indicate evangelicals are moving away from public schools and toward homeschooling or private Christian schools.[2] This is yet another example of a move away from efforts to bring widespread transformation to cultural institutions or attempting to utilize institutions run and controlled by others in favor of ownership. The creation of their own institutions gives evangelicals greater control over the values, mission, and content, though it may come at the cost of less direct cultural influence—at least in the short-term.

Without ownership of the core places, institutions, and platforms you rely on, you're exposed to potentially existential risk. Consider social media. Many people have built lucrative careers on social media platforms like YouTube or Instagram. But because they're using a platform owned by someone else, their livelihood and very digital presence can be erased at the click of a few keys or a change in an algorithm. Financial analyst Byrne Hobart described the fate of people in this situation when he wrote, "If you build a business on someone else's platform, in the end you're either doing R&D for features they'll add or you're setting yourself up to cede them your margins [profits]."[3]

When I began writing on Christian issues, I deliberately started with an emailed newsletter, which is still the core of what I do.[4] I own a list of my subscribers' email addresses, and I have it backed up on my computer and backup drives. My email software provider might choose to stop providing services to me, but because I own this list, I can turn to other companies that will. Had I decided to start with a YouTube channel, not only would I have had no idea who was watching my videos but no way to contact those people outside that system. And if YouTube chose to deplatform me, I would lose contact with almost all my followers.

Now I do have a YouTube channel and other social media of that kind, but I still focus heavily on my email list. Having a central channel to reach my followers and readers, where I own the relationship with them, is important in the world we live and work in today. I focus on developing that central channel for this reason.

One of the problems evangelicals face in America today is that they exist almost entirely inside space owned by others—legally owned in many cases, but more importantly, socially and culturally owned. This may include the places they work, shop, and dine. Evangelicals who live in urban centers are typically surrounded by people who overwhelmingly embrace secular progressive beliefs and perspectives, and they "own" the culture of that area.

Many businesses and residences in these places feature signs or flags that show their support of various causes embraced by secular progressives: pride flags, Black Lives Matter signs, or "In this house . . ." signs. Anyone who wants to display symbols that might be viewed as contrary to those causes may be made to feel unwelcome. For example, neighbors told a friend who lives near me in the Indianapolis area to take down his Betsy Ross flag. They claimed it was a "white nationalist" symbol.

Sometimes merely a refusal to display certain symbols—refusing to "wear the ribbon" as a well-known *Seinfeld* episode once put it[5]—can draw the ire of neighbors. A donut shop in my neighborhood was attacked and ultimately run out of business by activists demanding to know why the owners had not publicly supported Black Lives Matter and then launched a campaign to tar them as racists.[6]

Because of the growing challenges and pressures of the negative world environment, Christians will need to put more focus on acquiring ownership over many of the key aspects of our lives. I believe ownership will be increasingly important in three areas: economic, that is, scalable, wealth-generating businesses; social and cultural, especially "third place" gathering spots like coffee shops; and physical, that is to say, real estate.

ECONOMIC OWNERSHIP

Virtually all major corporations in America today have aggressively centered their firms around secular progressive ideologies.

This has been accomplished through various means, including the ESG (environmental, social, and governance) movement and the DEI (diversity, equity, inclusion) subcategory of ESG. Any publicly traded company—or nonpublic company funded by traditional venture capital or private equity—or one that depends on customers who are or relies on the government as a customer is now forced to adopt these ideologies because of a confluence of institutional pressures.

White-collar employees at these companies are especially exposed to ideological pressure. As Nassim Taleb put it in his book *Antifragile,*

> A midlevel banker with a mortgage would be fragile to the extreme. In fact, he would be completely a prisoner of the value system that invites him to be corrupt to the core—because of his dependence on the annual vacation in Barbados. The same with a civil servant in Washington.[7]

In my chapter 2 discussion of the challenges to the cultural engagement model in the negative world, I noted the particularly acute challenge facing people in prestigious professions. Traditional corporate or professional employment will continue to be a choice for many evangelicals who have the skills, inclination, and conscience that allow them to thrive in that environment. But we should also be working to create options for those who have the skills but aren't otherwise suited to work in these places. And in the years to come, opportunities in those fields for committed, evangelical Christians may be few and far between.

One way to develop alternative opportunities is for evangelicals to cultivate entrepreneurship, especially acquiring and maintaining ownership of privately held, medium-sized businesses not built with capital from traditional venture capital or private equity firms. I define medium-sized businesses, as is common, as those with revenue of more than $10 million per year but less than $1 billion per year.

These businesses are particularly important because they can generate significant wealth that can then be used to employ believers while creating financial resources to strengthen local evangelical churches and communities and fund missional work. They typically employ a significant number of people and need management and administrative capacity, which means the kind of white-collar jobs often missing from smaller businesses. And while many small businesses like restaurants pay low wages because they're economically marginal, medium-sized businesses often have good economics, which allow them to pay a living wage and provide quality benefits for their employees.

If they're located in a smaller city or suburb, these kinds of businesses are also likely to be major employers and taxpayers that local leaders can't afford to offend. A business that employs even just 250 people in a town of twenty-five thousand is a key pillar of that local economy. On the other hand, these companies are small enough that they're often able to operate under the radar and avoid the kinds of pressure and legal campaigns waged against evangelical-owned big businesses like Chick-fil-A and Hobby Lobby.

When a church has one or more congregants who privately own a medium-sized business like this, it provides a key source of financial support to that church, a source of jobs for congregants, and a potential safe temporary landing space for anyone who loses a corporate job. A profitable medium-sized business's financial ability to absorb an extra employee or two for a period of time can provide confidence and protection to those congregants who do work for the Fortune 500 company in town.

These medium-sized businesses can also implement an evangelical version of ESG: paying fair wages, delivering high-quality products and services, being honest in dealings with customers and suppliers and pursuing win-win relationships, hiring locally, investing in the local community, and creating a friendly environment for Christians to work in. Although it's a larger business, Chick-fil-A's policy of closing on Sunday is a good example of this in action. It not only honors Sabbath-keeping for Christians, but provides a guaranteed, predictable free weekend day off for all their employees.

In the next chapter, we'll take a closer look at how these kinds of business practices end up fueling mission and evangelism. But Maddox Industrial Transformer in Battle Ground, Washington, is an example of a medium-sized business doing this today.[8] CEO Camden Spiller and his brother privately own Maddox. Prior to owning the company, Spiller spent twenty years at another heavy industrial company, working his way up to become a junior partner in the enterprise. After the company was sold to a private equity firm, he saw firsthand the "cultural carnage" that resulted from the new ownership and soon found himself laid off from the firm where he'd previously been a part owner.

Spiller decided to start Maddox to disrupt the electrical transformer business. He wanted to make money, yes, but for him, starting a business was about more than just earning money for his own lifestyle or for traditional philanthropy. He said, "I wanted to be able to invest in people who are investing in building families, churches, and communities."

With the emergence of the negative world, Spiller also saw the need for Christian communities to control more of their own economic destiny. He believed the market for electrical infrastructure was a great place to be because it's a critical, essential service. "They gave us the road map with COVID," he said, referring to how essential businesses were allowed to continue operating during lockdowns. "We need to be in these essential businesses."

Maddox has been very successful, growing to over two hundred employees with annual revenue now reaching nine figures. The company has locations in Idaho, Ohio, South Carolina, Texas, and Washington State, and Maddox has been named to the prestigious Inc. 5000 fastest-growing companies in America list for four straight years.[9]

According to Spiller, they're working hard toward a goal of $1 billion in annual revenue. He thinks more Christian business owners should develop an expanded vision for what they can accomplish. As he put it, "You don't have to just be Mom and Pop to hold true to your values."

Spiller also didn't think he had to head for the hills to thrive as a Christian businessman. In fact, he intentionally moved to the Battle Ground area, part of the greater Portland metropolitan area, to start his business. His wife had grown up there, so there were family ties, but he also saw the value of being part of a major metropolitan center. Maddox's headquarters is only twenty minutes from the Portland airport, for example. Rather than operating in fear-driven retreat, he went on the advance by moving to the secular progressive Pacific Northwest area.

The cash Maddox generated has enabled investment in other ventures. The Spillers purchased seventy acres of land right off downtown Battle Ground, where they intend to build, among other things, a new building for their growing church. But the space is also intended for several new ventures that will help him diversify his holdings as well as build up the local economy. Spiller notes that he would love to see an ecosystem of other businesses like Maddox developed there.

Medium-sized companies like Maddox can be a tentpole enterprise for a local church or Christian community. Building these kinds of enterprises without using sources of financing that would impose ESG-type policies and then retaining ownership for the long-term is difficult. And so this kind of entrepreneurship isn't for everyone. But it will be an increasing necessity for at least some evangelicals to start more businesses like these in order to strengthen their communities so they can withstand the pressures of the negative world.

Of course, a Christian community becoming over-reliant on a single company like Maddox comes with its own risks. So having multiple entrepreneurs in a local church or Christian community reduces that risk, even if not all of them are as large as Maddox. Churches themselves may also want to engage in for-profit activities to generate revenue. In *The Coming Revolution in Church Economics*, Mark DeYmaz and Harry Li argue that churches can no longer rely on only tithes and offerings and should seek to develop multiple revenue streams, including from for-profit activities like facilities rental and church-owned businesses.[10] While in the negative world, churches should be cautious about the kinds of risk exposure they might incur from engaging in business, DeYmaz and Li correctly encourage churches and Christians to adopt an entrepreneurial mindset.

SOCIAL AND CULTURAL OWNERSHIP

I highlight the critical importance of medium-sized businesses achieving economic ownership, but we can't forget small businesses, especially because of their ability to create social and culturally owned space in our local communities. Small businesses can create establishments that are Christian friendly even if they aren't explicitly Christian and provide a valuable resource to the community.

As noted earlier, many retail establishments today, even on small-town courthouse squares in rural counties, prominently display various secular progressive symbols. Coffee shops and independently owned bookstores are especially known for this, and in urban areas, displaying these signs or markers is virtually a requirement to stay in business. Those who don't agree to display them risk being driven out of business amid a growing sense that these displays mark that territory as culturally owned by the values of secular progressivism.

But obstacles like this also provide an opportunity. When evangelical entrepreneurs open high-quality retail shops, coffee shops, and restaurants, this not only provides an opportunity for Christians to have culturally owned space but provides a much-needed alternative for the entire community. This doesn't necessarily mean putting up overtly Christian or culturally conservative displays, or that the business should be conceived of as a ministry. Personally, I'm not all that interested in having to navigate these types of displays of any ideological variety just to get a simple cup of coffee. In our overly politicized world, providing a place that is simply depoliticized or neutral can be an oasis for many people.

In other words, a Christian-owned coffee shop does not have to be explicitly Christian to be a well-run coffee shop valued by the community. It can simply be an ordinary, locally owned café with a good design that serves excellent coffee. People will patronize it for its quality, not the religious background of its owner.

An example of such a Christian-owned coffee shop is Indie Coffee Roasters in the Indianapolis suburb of Carmel, founded by a former pastor. But the same logic extends beyond coffee shops. Honest Mary's restaurant in Austin, Texas, was founded by a Christian. Lazarus Brewing in the same city was founded by a Presbyterian pastor. Philanthropy Fashions is a

Christian-owned retailer in the Nashville suburb of Franklin. Christians may want to run many varieties of small businesses like these.

Although not a for-profit business, the F3 workout movement—F3 stands for fitness, fellowship, and faith—is another good example. These are peer-led morning men's workout groups designed to promote friendships among men in a world where men too often lack friends, as well as to provide a space for men to pray with one another.[11] To be clear, F3 is not a Christian ministry—participants can be of any religion—but it is certainly a Christian friendly workout environment.

These sorts of businesses aren't always easy to start. Small business is notoriously difficult and has a high failure rate. As noted earlier, ownership of retail or "third place"–type businesses like coffee shops can still be difficult in extremely secular progressive neighborhoods. Some today believe "silence is violence" and to be apolitical makes you an enemy. Acquiring social and cultural ownership will not be equally viable everywhere. But it's still viable in many places, especially where secular progressives are a minority of the population yet are overrepresented in retail businesses, like small town or suburban Main Streets.

PHYSICAL OWNERSHIP

When most Christians think about real estate ownership in relation to their faith, they traditionally think about owning a church building or perhaps, in the context of personal financial stewardship, a family seeking to pay off their mortgage and own their own home. As we transition into the negative world, we need to think more broadly about real estate.

In past decades, we witnessed the rise of the evangelical

megachurch—large, multi-building campuses designed to accommodate thousands of people. But when it comes to traditional church campuses in the negative world, evangelicals might want to be less ambitious.

A big church building, potentially with a big mortgage, creates fragility and limits the options that church has financially. While churches may never lose their tax exemptions, if that were to happen, it could cause serious problems for the ones with high levels of debt seeking to maintain an expensive building. Similarly, churches with large debt can't as easily afford to lose members and might face pressure from larger donors on a particular theological issue. Just as with individuals, staying leaner as a congregation helps churches stay stronger in the face of pressures.

That's not to say churches shouldn't own buildings or should build cheap structures. But for long-term future planning, the additional risks of the negative world need to be taken into account.

On the other hand, evangelicals might want to be even more aggressive where some real estate opportunities exist. Ownership of real estate can help sustain long-term community.

Twenty to thirty years ago, the neighborhood where I live in Indianapolis, greater Fountain Square, was a decaying area crying out for investment. A local nonprofit community development corporation (CDC) started building and rehabbing houses to try to help neighborhood renters become homeowners. But that process was moving slowly, so Bill Taft, the CDC's executive director at the time, made a pitch to members of his new downtown church plant, asking them to consider buying in the area and therefore investing in the city. This was long before urban living was popular in Indianapolis.

A number of people in that church community bought homes in this neighborhood, and as a result, several key streets now have a critical mass of Christian homeowners committed to living in and serving the area for the long-term. Being close to one another provides strong, deep community in a neighborhood that is otherwise heavily secular, and they also became the core of a new Presbyterian church there.

These believers are also committed to working for the overall benefit and betterment of the whole neighborhood, not just being urban consumers. And because they bought their homes long before urban living took off here, they haven't been displaced by the increase in real estate prices that developed when others started flocking back to the city.

Perhaps the most impressive accomplishment in Christian real estate ownership is in Moscow, Idaho, where members, businesses, and institutions associated with the very conservative Christ Church have acquired a significant amount of property on and around Main Street. Contrary to the stereotype of Idaho as a far-right redoubt of survivalist compounds, Moscow is a college town, home to the University of Idaho, the state's flagship university. Conservative Christians there have acquired a significant portion of the city's main commercial street.

This physical space enables Christ Church to maintain a visible presence in the community center, comprising the campus of their church, a Christian university, and a media company. People associated with the church also run a coffee shop and gastropub on Main Street.[12] This ownership of space makes them extremely difficult, if not impossible, to displace.

Ownership of assets—institutions like schools, our economic life, social and cultural space, and even real estate—will be increasingly important for evangelicals in a world where the mainstream institutions of society are both degrading in their competence and increasingly hostile toward evangelical values. Acquiring complete ownership over everything isn't possible, of course. But some ownership can help provide a form of community—and not just individual resiliency.

While every community is different, and not everybody is equally able to acquire ownership in every domain, those engaged in thinking and planning for the future of Christian life and witness in the United States need to look for ways to be less dependent on secular institutions. Ownership is a key dimension of that. Ownership of property and businesses also allows their evangelical owners to promote genuine community flourishing. These investments sustain property values, employ fellow citizens, and generate tax revenue for local governments. And as we will see in the next chapter, in some cases they can even create platforms for ministry.

PART FOUR

ENGAGING
MISSIONALLY

CHAPTER 10

BE A LIGHT

DURING A TRIP TO SEE FAMILY IN MY HOMETOWN, I heard the pastor in the church I grew up attending tell the congregation about an incident a few days earlier. He was in his office when he saw a car pull into the church parking lot. But no one got out, so after a few minutes he walked outside and found a woman and her children sitting there.

He asked if he could help them somehow, and the woman said, "I've been off drugs three days, but I'm not going to make it, and I heard you can get help here." My old pastor said how glad he was that their church was known to people out there in the world as a place they could turn to for help.

This story is certainly not unique, and it's just one example among many of how the church serves as a beacon of light in a dark world—a place where you can still go for help. In a country where life expectancy has been declining, we're witnessing record numbers of opioid overdose deaths. Nobel Prize–winning economists are talking about "deaths of despair,"[1] young people are expressing their unhappiness over the dysfunctions of dating apps,[2] politics have become viciously polarized, and even basic biological reality about gender is denied.

Today, then, perhaps more than ever in our lifetime, the church must be a light. Above all, it must be a light that shares and witnesses to the gospel of Jesus Christ. As Mark Jobe, senior pastor at New Life Community Church in Chicago and president of Moody Bible Institute, put it, "Wherever you find extremes of dysfunction, you also find great opportunities for the light of Jesus to be able to shine even stronger."[3]

The negative world not only brings new pressures to bear on American evangelicals but opens new possibilities for mission and evangelism. Taking advantage of these opportunities will require expanding our repertoire of tools, especially in performing the critical task of pre-evangelism in new ways.

When Billy Graham started holding crusades in the mid-twentieth-century era, he could assume that those listening had a basic familiarity with Christianity. He didn't have to explain who Jesus Christ is, for example. In the positive world era, even as the social status of Christianity was on the decline, the developers of the seeker sensitivity model were able to take advantage of this basic familiarity with and friendliness to Christianity. At some level many people knew they should be Christians, even if they presently weren't. Bill Hybels's survey question asking people why they didn't go to church presumed much of this background.

Then with the transition to the neutral world, the background conditions for traditional evangelism and outreach faded in much of the country. And today, with the emergence of the negative world, that decline is far advanced. This means the cultural conditions for evangelism have changed and we're in what some have referred to as a post-Christian culture.[4] Conveying the truths to Christianity today, then, is more akin to the work of a cross-cultural missionary introducing the gospel for the first time to a foreign culture. A significant amount of pre-evangelism is necessary to prepare the way for someone to understand and respond to what we're sharing.

The "He Gets Us" advertising campaign,[5] which launched in 2022 and continues as I write, may end up spending $1 billion[6] and is an example of an attempt at this type of pre-evangelism. Haven, the advertising firm that developed it, did a significant amount of market research to understand people's knowledge of Jesus. Bill McKendry, founder and chief creative officer of the firm, said, "We found out that there's a wide swath of people in the United States that think they know a lot about Jesus, but when you start scratching the surface, they really don't know."[7] The campaign was designed with the goal of introducing Jesus and portraying him as relatable to the modern American.

This campaign immediately generated controversy and has drawn criticism from both evangelicals[8] and non-Christians.[9] But whatever people think of it, it's targeted at a legitimate need some evangelicals today don't even recognize—namely, the need for pre-evangelism. This campaign isn't trying to share the gospel message; it's attempting to introduce Jesus to people in a positive way to prepare them for future evangelism. In a negative world, this type of introduction to Jesus—in a variety of different ways—is an important activity, one that every Christian will need to learn how to do.

The need for pre-evangelism reveals the price today's Christians must pay for the loss of so-called cultural Christianity. Some evangelicals, like Russell Moore[10] or pastor Ray Ortlund,[11] have criticized and even celebrated the downfall of cultural Christianity (sometimes called "Bible Belt Christianity" or other terms). They rightly have noted that cultural Christianity doesn't save people and can give them a false sense of eternal security or even make them self-righteous.

But cultural Christianity had some benefits as well, as it could incline people to be receptive to the gospel because they assumed Christianity to be true. And it provided the background context in which the sharing of the gospel would be comprehensible to most people. The decline of Christianity since the 1960s, however, has created a different world and highlighted the pressing need for evangelicals to undertake the pre-evangelism that cultural Christianity previously did for them. To do this on a large scale is likely to be difficult and costly as the $1 billion price tag of the He Gets Us campaign illustrates. But campaigns like this aren't the only way to engage in pre-evangelism.

The need for new forms of evangelistic outreach is just one example of how the negative world has further increased the challenges of being a Christian in America. To be sure, the degree of challenge you face as a follower of Christ will differ greatly depending on your context. In the negative world, even some legacy approaches from the positive and neutral worlds will continue to work for some people in some contexts. Direct preaching of the gospel will continue to reach many people. Perhaps they were raised in Christian homes, previously attended church, live in an area of the country that is still positive toward Christianity, or have experienced some other form of pre-evangelism. And of course, there's always the reality that the moving of the Holy Spirit can overcome any barrier to quicken hearts to faith and make people ready to respond.

Service to the community, like helping the poor and the suffering, is itself a form of pre-evangelism. The church has a strong record in helping people who are struggling with problems in life. America is blanketed with churches and Christian ministries that help the homeless, feed the hungry, clothe the poor, minister to the drug addict or prisoner. Nothing reveals people's spiritual need for a Savior more than hard times in their earthly lives, and many turn to Jesus only after hitting the proverbial rock bottom.

So while evangelicals should continue many of their current

forms of evangelistic outreach, the negative world highlights the need for new forms of pre-evangelism that must be developed specifically for the negative world. What's new is not just that Christianity is unknown, but that it has low status. Negative world strategies need to provide a message that's attractive to people despite the status messages sent by society.

The good news is that we can do this. And indeed, it's already being done in some cases. Consider the work the church is specifically doing to help struggling drug addicts, for example.[12] People desperate to escape addiction are less likely to worry about whether being associated with Jesus will make them seem uncool, and the church has answers to the problems a world that rejects Christ can't solve. It has truth that won't otherwise be heard in a world that too often promotes lies, a shining light in a world of darkness.

In this chapter I highlight three emerging strategies we can emphasize and develop to be a light that guides people to the gospel—even in a negative world: speaking truth clearly, creating healthy communities, and building trustworthy enterprises.

THE LIGHT OF CLARITY ON TRUTH

In the positive and even in the neutral world, society at large still accepted what C. S. Lewis called the Tao—the natural law of God's created order. Even where people in secular society explicitly rejected God's law, they often showed at least some consideration for it. In the 1990s, President Clinton famously said he wanted abortion to be "safe, legal, and rare."[13] Whatever his personal, private beliefs may have been, even a president who believed abortion should be legal still publicly proclaimed that it was at least in some sense tragic, ideally to be avoided in most cases.

Today, people are encouraged to "shout your abortion"[14] and actively affirm abortion as a moral good. Once viewed as tragic, abortion is now seen as a means of exercising autonomy and expressing individual identity and values.

Again, and similarly, we see how many people today de facto deny the biological reality of gender. A recent article in the *London Review of Books* said:

> Others take the gold standard for the identification of sex to be chromosomes—incontrovertible evidence, written into the very code of our cells, of who each of us really is. Yet most of us will never know anything of our chromosomes. . . . We know even less of the chromosomes, gonads, hormones and genitals of others. What we register are hair and clothes and whatever can be discerned of fat and muscles. Almost all of these markers are readily modified through dieting, exercise, depilation, surgery, hormones and make-up.[15]

And in March 2022, looking confused when asked what a woman is at her confirmation hearing, Supreme Court justice nominee Ketanji Brown Jackson answered, "I'm not a biologist." A *USA Today* headline read, "Marsha Blackburn asked Ketanji Brown Jackson to define 'woman.' Science says there's no simple answer."[16] *No simple answer.*

This new world produces opportunities for mission and evangelism by bringing clarity regarding the truth—that which corresponds to reality, or as the apostle Paul characterized it, that which is "clearly seen" or when people "do by nature things required by the law."[17] In the positive and neutral worlds, key strategies for mission sought to evangelize by reducing what their practitioners saw as artificial barriers to the gospel message. The seeker sensitivity approach sought to eliminate anything that would turn people away from church, like stodgy hymns and old liturgies. The cultural engagement approach wanted to avoid provocative rhetoric, anything that would turn people off by emphasizing culture war issues in favor of what they believed was a more gospel-centered approach, keeping the focus on Jesus so as not to be distracted by peripheral matters.

As we shift to recognizing the negative world, we must also recognize that these approaches have lost some of their effectiveness, and if the church fails to adapt to the new cultural context, we may miss potentially large opportunities to reach the lost. Consider, for example, the well-publicized problem the church has reaching men. This has long been known and discussed, yet millions of young males continue to turn to secular men's gurus like Jordan Peterson, not the church, for answers and advice. Why? In part because Peterson is willing to speak truth to them clearly and compellingly.

I say more on this in the next chapter, but one of Peterson's attractive features was his willingness to forthrightly state that differences between men and women exist and that he would refuse to comply with state mandates to use certain pronouns, among other things. This type of bold yet not gratuitously offensive honesty is attractive to those who are hungry for truth and tired of ignoring what is plainly known and clearly perceived.

While in the negative world there's a social cost to speaking the truth plainly, we should also consider who we're not reaching by failing to speak the truth clearly. As theologian and pastor James Wood said in criticizing an excessive focus on "winsomeness" in certain parts of the evangelical world, "We are missing opportunities here. There are tons of people in the middle of the cultural storms who are crying out for someone to speak clearly, to be a courageous voice of reason . . . There are evangelistic opportunities here that we should not miss."[18]

Wood also notes that minimizing parts of the Christian message to avoid alienating some people creates its own set of problems:

> On top of this, avoiding clear teachings on the hot-button issues of our days is also foolish. If you mute hard teachings to get persons in the door, you set up a likelihood that you will mute them indefinitely. As A.W. Tozer said: "You win them *to* what you win them *with*." People don't like to feel that they have been had—that you pulled something on them, tricked them to get them in the door and then later bring up the offensive things in your pastoral shepherding.[19]

Progressive author Jen Hatmaker agreed with this, posting similar sentiments on social media, saying she had more respect for churches that were transparently not LGBTQ-affirming than those who tried to disguise or minimize their stance through "all are welcome" type rhetoric.

> It is the "friendly, welcoming churches" that shatter LGBTQ hearts more. The ones that hug gay couples and have "All are welcome" slogans. The ones that emulate a wide front door but are quietly breaking LGBTQ people behind the curtain: denying them the right to lead, preach, serve, mentor, chaperone, host, marry. It's gut-wrenching, and they limp into our sanctuary constantly, betrayed and denied by their friendly, welcoming churches. Those places break people, neither hot nor cold, just basking in the glow of lukewarm friendliness that cuts like a knife after you get past the front door.[20]

Evangelical churches must have a firm resolve as to what they believe to be true and then have the courage to speak it clearly. This doesn't mean giving gratuitous offense or being a provocateur. While Jordan Peterson has made an unfortunately more political and confrontational turn of late, he wasn't trying to give offense when he first became well known. Standing on and speaking the truth was more important to him than avoiding conflict, and that drew millions of young men to him like moths to a flame.

Trying to cleverly nuance certain issues to avoid offense will no longer offer protection against the ire of secular society in the negative world. And worse, it risks obscuring the truth. This will increasingly be a barrier to effective evangelization.

THE LIGHT OF HEALTHY COMMUNITIES

A Christian community that's living in truth with healthy patterns of life and relationship among individuals, families, and throughout the corporate life of the church will also be a light to the surrounding culture. In chapter 8 I talked about the necessity of repairing our own sexual economy in the church. This is an important element of strengthening our own communities, but it's also about the church having something that people are struggling to find for themselves.

For instance, many people have intentionally rejected marriage and chosen not to have children. But others want marriage and children; they just can't figure out how to get them in today's world. They've lost a narrative that leads to health and happiness and are looking for a new pathway, preferably one that others have trod and has visible evidence of success.

The simple act of building healthy Christian families in churches where marriage with children is the norm will be increasingly countercultural in the negative world. Yet doing this will demonstrate that it's not only possible but provides evidence of a different way for people to live their lives.

Evangelicals, then, should be willing to help others find this way of life for themselves instead of affirming them in choices that take them further from where they want to go. But to do it in a way that isn't condescending or communicated with a judgmental spirit. As with helping people who are experiencing other forms of suffering, this also provides a platform for sharing the gospel.

When my wife and I lived in New York City, we sometimes invited singles to our apartment for dinner. Not only was this an opportunity to spend time together, but a way to share our family life with and provide an extended community to our single friends in a city where community is notoriously hard to find. It was also an opportunity for them to have a window into the choices we made and the priorities we were living by.

During numerous conversations my wife had with non-Christian women in New York, the women were surprised when she told them we hadn't lived together or had sex before marriage. What was even more surprising was how much they approved of our decision, including one woman who had just moved in with her boyfriend. Even applying a gracious discount to this—after all, we tend not to mock other people's choices to their faces—the responses seemed so genuinely enthusiastic that my wife was taken aback.

Some people have even written publicly about their pull toward values foreign to them. One secular feminist admitted she was "obsessed" with Mormon mommy blogs, writing, "Their lives are nothing like mine—I'm your standard-issue late-20-something childless overeducated atheist feminist—yet I'm completely obsessed with their blogs . . . I'm not alone, either."[21]

Many people simply don't believe it's possible to get

married without first living together or at least having premarital sex. But it very much can be done, and that "old-fashioned" approach still has something compelling about it, even if many people would never admit it publicly. Evangelicals who embrace a Christian sexual ethic and courageously live it out publicly let people see not only how but why they're doing it.

In my mind, the bigger problem is that too often evangelicals *aren't* living out a Christian sexual ethic. And even when they do, too many hide their successful families under a bushel either to avoid making others feel bad or because they fear they'll be mocked for being different.

As with speaking the truth, letting healthy families and communities be a light won't necessarily be popular. Just consider the criticism directed at former Vice President Mike Pence for taking basic precautions to protect his marriage, such as not attending events where alcohol is served unless accompanied by his wife.[22] But never underestimate how attractive countercultural living can be to women stuck on the Tinder treadmill or to men who believe they are forever doomed to being an outcast "incel" (an "involuntary celibate" or a man who receives no interest from women).[23]

In the early church, the attractiveness of the Christian lifestyle in contrast to the pagan one was, even by its pagan critics, cited as a factor in its spread. In his Letter to Arsacius, Emperor Julian the Apostate wrote, "Why, then, do we think that this is enough, why do we not observe that it is their [Christians] benevolence to strangers, their care for the graves of the dead and the pretended holiness of their lives that have done most to increase atheism [rejection of the Roman gods]?"[24]

Today, it probably won't be evangelical funerals that attract people. But the very way we live as Christians and as the church can by itself be a light. It can provide a vision of what healthy family and community life looks like. This can and should include showing how single people participate in and are valued as part of the life of the church.

But being a light in this way is possible only by living in a fundamentally different and better way than the world lives. If evangelicals are conformed to unhealthy secular patterns of life, with the same basic number of single people, divorces, and so on the world has, then there is no light to put on the lampstand. In an ever more dysfunctional and toxic society, tasks like repairing our own sexual economy are thus directly related to evangelism and mission.

THE LIGHT OF TRUSTWORTHY ENTERPRISES

Another source of light is the way evangelicals conduct affairs in the world, such as acting with integrity and trustworthiness, engaging in honest marketing, delivering what we promise, offering high-quality products and services, avoiding dishonest tactics like the bait and switch, and owning and correcting mistakes when we make them.

The decline of trust in institutions is an example of how America is transitioning from what was once a high-trust society to a much lower-trust one. For example, when I was growing up in the 1980s, many people still left their doors unlocked, and in some cases they even left their keys in the car. Virtually nobody does that today, not even in my rural Indiana hometown.

We see this decline in trust in the business world too. Rather than being governed by ethical principles in which certain things are simply not done or viewed as unseemly, today business leaders too often do whatever they can get away with. Laws that used to protect the weak, such as those against charging excessive interest, prohibiting gambling, or consuming certain drugs like marijuana, have been repealed. Companies have surged into areas that used to be the province of shady characters like the mafia, only now they're doing business and making profits on an industrial scale.

Legal consequences for criminal actions by connected corporate CEOs have all but disappeared. In the S&L crisis of the 1980s, more than eight hundred people were convicted of federal crimes. During the dot-com era, executives at companies like Enron and WorldCom were sentenced to lengthy prison terms. During the financial crash of the 2007 to 2009 era, by contrast, only one banker went to jail.[25] Not long ago, Wells Fargo Bank created millions of accounts that customers never requested, but no one was ever prosecuted, and the bank itself got off by paying a fine.[26] A poor single mother who writes a bad check faces more legal risk than a too-big-to-fail bank CEO committing industrial-scale fraud.

Every day in the newspaper there's another story about corporate malfeasance. The *New York Times* reported, for example, that America's major insurance companies were defrauding Medicare by aggressively and inappropriately coding patients as sicker than they really were.[27] The *Times* also reported on how supposedly nonprofit hospitals were sending debt collectors after patients who were legally entitled to free care.[28]

During the twentieth century, laws and regulations were put in place to set and enforce standards for worker safety, food safety, and truth in advertising. Prior to that, it had been a Wild West era for business. In that environment, some Christian businessmen in nineteenth-century Victorian Britain, the Quakers, were able to set themselves apart in the market. They were extremely successful in business, and one reason was that in an era when most businesses couldn't be trusted, people knew Quaker-run ones were trustworthy.

In a look at the originally Quaker business Cadbury chocolate, the *London Review of Books* observed,

> In Victorian Britain, Quaker businessmen had compet-
> itive advantages. Ron Davies, in his biography of George
> Stephenson (Quakers were early financiers of the railways),
> talks about a Quaker "moral mafia." In a commercial
> landscape filled with fraudsters and dodgy dealers, non-
> Quakers liked doing business with the Friends, knowing the
> extraordinary lengths the community would go to vet its
> members' entrepreneurial ventures and, if things went sour,
> to prevent, or make good, the consequences of bad loans
> and bankruptcy. As for the workforce, Robert Fitzgerald, in
> his account of the Rowntrees, points out that since "busi-
> ness and wealth were viewed by the Quakers as a God-given
> trust, labour could not be treated as a mere commodity."[29]

According to that article, in the nineteenth century, other
chocolate companies regularly mixed in materials like brick dust
and iron filings to minimize cost. Cadbury never did that. Not
only did they thrive, then, but the company grew to be a corporate giant and brand that's still powerful in the market today.
There's an old quip about Pennsylvania—that the Quakers there
came to do good and ended up doing well. But it's possible to do
both. Of course, the legacy Quaker businesses in the UK aren't
what they once were. The originally Quaker Barclays Bank has
become one of the most scandal-prone in Britain.[30]

Today's situation is also very different from the nineteenth
century. Yet we, too, are in a declining trust environment in
the negative world. How far trust ultimately declines and what
the public consequences of that will be are yet to be deter-
mined. But perhaps there will be both business and missional
opportunities here simply by being a trustworthy actor.

As general societal trust declines, people will need compen-sating structures to mitigate the negative consequences of living in a lower-trust society. This will mean, for example, building a network of people who can be trusted, such as family and close friends. These are the very things people increasingly don't have today. It also means finding businesses and insti-tutions that people can trust, and Christian-owned businesses can be those trustworthy entities people can rely on.

My dentist is a Christian and a longtime reader and sup-porter of my work. My electrician doesn't advertise himself as the "Christian electrician," but he does note his church affil-iation on his website. When I lived in Rhode Island, my auto mechanic was a fellow member of my church. All these people have provided first-rate service to me.

But there's also a missional component here. When Christian-owned firms like these are operating successfully, and with integrity and Christian values, that creates a light of trustworthiness in a world of declining trust. It gives people a reason to see Christians in a positive light and think positively about at least some aspects of Christianity. So like helping the poor or other traditional social service ministry, this can serve as a form of pre-evangelism.

It can also provide a more direct platform for mission. Simply conducting your business with high integrity is a coun-tercultural witness in a world that doesn't recognize objective moral standards. Treating workers fairly is missional in a world where labor is viewed purely as a commodity. And as Camden Spiller, the CEO I profiled in chapter 9 said, "Work relationships provide an opportunity to mentor people in a different way," than a pastor can. When an employee has serious problems that threaten their job, a boss has an ability to encourage them to get help and make a change—an abil-ity a pastor, family member, or social friend may not have.

There's also a kind of *esprit de corps* that comes from working together, creating relational space to speak into other people's lives.

All these touch points are potential opportunities for sharing the gospel and talking about faith. And while it's easy to adopt a defensive, doom-and-gloom attitude toward secular dysfunction, this approach also provides opportunities to engage in mission through the way Christians and Christian institutions conduct themselves in the world.

The negative world brings new challenges for the church, but it also creates new opportunities for mission and evangelism. We can provide clarity on truth in a world where people are required to profess the absurd. We can model a healthier way of living for people who are looking for something better than what the world is giving them. And we can conduct our affairs in a way that aligns with our Christian convictions and is markedly different from the way business is too often done today.

All of these will create an attractive light even in a world where Christianity—and Christians—are seen as lower status. These areas of focus are pre-evangelistic in that they draw people's attention to the church and provide a platform for the actual sharing of the gospel. As evangelicals restructure their lives, churches, and institutions to adapt to the negative world, this should include thinking about how to mobilize to take advantage of these new opportunities for mission by being a light in the world.

CHAPTER 11

BE A SOURCE
OF TRUTH

ONE OF SOVIET DISSIDENT ALEKSANDR SOLZHENITSYN'S most famous essays is titled "Live Not by Lies."[1] In it he recognized that it wasn't always possible for citizens under communism to openly speak the truth, but at least they could refuse to say things they knew to be untrue. Yet even the act of refusing to give assent to lies, Solzhenitsyn acknowledged, might cause hardship such as loss of employment, and it would pose special challenges for young people. But he recognized the criticality of upholding the truth in enacting resistance to an unjust government.

Thankfully, America today—even in the negative world—is not the communist tyranny of the Soviet Union. But ideological lines to which its people must give their assent do exist. It's also a world where the truth is very much in question. Can the official pronouncements of scientists, government officials, or other authority figures be trusted? The decline of trust in institutions and the rise of conspiracy theories suggests people are losing faith in those authorities and institutions, skeptical that they're reliably giving us the truth.

When top public health officials like the Surgeon General tell people to "stop buying masks" during a pandemic[2] and then implement widespread mask mandates, people naturally question whether what they're being told is true. This is similar to when they observe politicians like Barack Obama say they oppose same-sex marriage on account of their Christian faith and then immediately celebrate it once it's legalized.[3] Or when they're told "weapons of mass destruction" exist in Iraq and a full-scale invasion is launched, only to later be told there weren't a significant number of such weapons there after all, they wonder whether the intelligence world was mistaken as claimed or they'd been lied to or at the very least misled from the beginning.

People are hungry for the truth today, and evangelicals must be able and willing to be that source of truth in a negative world, even when their traditional, historic beliefs accord them lower social status.

It's easy, and all too common, for evangelicals to look outward at the world and complain about its untruths. But we must also have the courage to look inward to see where evangelicalism itself has been wrong. In some areas, evangelicals have been mistaken—honestly mistaken, perhaps, but mistaken nevertheless.

In other areas, overly simplistic views of the world have shaped evangelical teachings. I believe one key reason for this is that evangelicals have relied too much on pastors as general-purpose guides to the world, a role they're often ill-equipped to perform. A critical task for Christian believers in the negative world is to discern and courageously realign ourselves fully with the truth. This is both for us and in order to share that truth with the world.

But our leaders can't fix this by themselves. It will require developing genuine expertise and training and leadership development among those who aren't full-time staff or vocational church leaders. We need a broad, well-equipped lay leadership active at the grassroots level.

EVANGELICALS AND GENDER

There are certainly several areas where evangelical teachings may need to be rethought. In this chapter, I'll focus on one specific area where I'm convinced the evangelical world needs to revisit its teachings: the way we teach on gender. Gender is arguably one of the key flashpoint issues in our culture, and untruths about it are foundational to the secular ideologies of the negative world. This topic is an example of the rethinking that needs to be done in other areas too.

I started writing about Christian topics in areas of particular interest to men. A decade ago, I was already seeing young men turning to online influencers and secular men's gurus in droves, looking for guidance in life there, not in the church. As I mentioned earlier, it has long been known that the church has struggled to attract men.[4] But the rising influence of these gurus shows that men aren't detached and disinterested; they're looking for someone to guide them in life. They just aren't looking to the church or its leaders for that guidance.

When I started writing about these topics, many of these secular influencers had hundreds of thousands of followers, but few Americans could name a single one of them. Today, almost everyone has heard of superstars like the aforementioned Jordan Peterson and Joe Rogan. The stark contrast between evangelical frustration on the one hand and the success of secular men's gurus on the other is one of evangelicalism's great missional failures.

Incidentally, the same is arguably true for women. Many

women are also looking to secular online influencers for direction. While I recognize this, I'll be focusing primarily on men
because it's the area I'm most familiar with.

Let's get one thing straight upfront: when millions of young
men turn to these gurus instead of to the church, that doesn't
mean the church is wrong. It could be, as Christ himself said,
that some people prefer the darkness to the light (John 3:19).
And while some of these secular men's gurus, like Peterson, are
fairly anodyne figures, many others have immoral and noxious
views.

The pick-up artist community is one of them, for example.
And the incel, or involuntarily celibate, community has
inspired multiple acts of terrorism.[5] Many who advocate for
a hedonistic or Nietzschean approach to life are also drawing
large audiences.[6] Popularity doesn't mean someone is speaking truth or teaching in accord with Christian morality, and
at least part of some of these figures' success is because they
promote ungodly lifestyles that many young men simply prefer
to lead.

Yet I believe many young men today are attracted to these
gurus and teachers for other reasons as well. And to a significant extent, these online secular men's gurus are popular
because, although morally wrong in many ways, they're providing factual and useful information. In fact, young men come
to them because they're saying something true—and in some
cases they're giving more true and useful information than the
typical evangelical church is. This needs to change. What's true
is always more important than what's popular.

Most gender discussions in the evangelical world center on
disputes between the "egalitarian"[7] and "complementarian"[8]
camps. Egalitarians hold that men and women are equally
made in the image of God, and that while there may be some
complementary differences between them, all roles in life are

equally open to women and men. They teach that women can be pastors and that men and women have equal decision-making weight in the home.

Complementarians also believe that men and women are equally made in the image of God and that there are some complementary differences between them, but they believe the role of church elder or pastor is reserved for men, and that men are called by God to be the head of the home.

Within complementarianism, a further division between "thin" and "thick" complementarians is made. Thin complementarians tend to take a minimalist stance on gender differences, focusing on male-only eldership and men being the head of the home, but otherwise stressing the similarities of the sexes and the equal openness of all other roles in life to women. Thick complementarians emphasize a more substantive gender complementarity, arguing that women should be more focused on the home or that they should potentially not enter certain professions.[9]

These are important debates, but because they tend to focus on a narrow range of issues related to the church, they tend to overlook significant parts of life and many of the most critical challenges men and women face in today's twenty-first-century world.

Here's a simple example of what I mean. One of the most well-known and widely established facts in social science is that women initiate the vast majority of divorces—around 70 percent of them. The exact percentage varies depending on the source, but there's no doubt about that general conclusion.[10]

I've listened to a large variety of evangelical sermons on marriage and have read a number of evangelical books and articles on this topic, and never have I seen a pastor give this basic information—not even in books that are otherwise filled with statistics. I'm sure some evangelical leaders have at least mentioned this fact, but it's certainly not commonly encountered in church circles.

The answer to why there's such a significant gender skew in filing for divorce is not as clear-cut. It is not my intent to argue here that this indicates lower marital commitment by women, greater levels of bad behavior by men, or any other explanation. But the fact that pastors aren't considering this information as part of their teachings on gender and marriage discredits the church as a reliable source of information on the topic. Conversely, it credentializes the online men's gurus who do very much put this type of data front and center when they speak on gender matters.

DIFFERENCES BETWEEN
THE TWO GENDERS

In some other areas, evangelicals don't ignore the facts but may fail to develop them or underemphasize them. The differences between the two genders is one of those. Online men's gurus directly say there is substantive complementarity between men and women. That is, they freely acknowledge that men and women are pervasively different on a wide range of characteristics.[11] One thing that made Jordan Peterson a sensation was his appearance on the UK's Channel 4, when he held his ground against a hostile questioner in describing the significant differences between the sexes, such as the personality trait of agreeableness.[12] As a PhD psychologist, Peterson is well versed in the academic literature here and quite competent in explaining these points.

One such area of difference is in the dating behaviors of men and women. The rise of online dating has provided immense amounts of hard, quantitative data about the behavior of each gender in the dating market. What they do when looking for someone on OkCupid or Tinder may not be the same as what they would do in trying to meet someone in a real-world venue. But with online dating now being the leading way couples meet, it's more important than ever to understand how people behave on these sites. Again, this can be measured objectively through data science. And what do we find? The data shows us significant differences between male and female behavior.

In one study, OkCupid showed that younger women prefer slightly older men, and older women prefer slightly younger men, but most women say that a man around their own age looks best to them. Men, by contrast and no matter what their age, view women in their early twenties as most attractive.[13] This is challenging for older women.

But another OkCupid study, on the distribution of attraction, came up with results that might surprise you. Men tend to rate an individual woman's attractiveness on a bell-type curve, with most rated average and then tapering to the extremes. By contrast, women tend to rate 7 percent of men as above average in looks and 81 percent of men as below average.[14] So studies of online dating that use the same types of statistics used to measure income inequality in the economy have found that men face significantly more dating inequality than women, a level equivalent to some of the most unequal economies in the world.[15]

My point is not to make a case for what evangelical churches should teach on gender, but rather to point out that what is attractive about these online gurus is their use of data-based, factual information to explain what's happening in the world. And the explanations they provide accord with lived experience for many young men. These online gurus are well versed in this data, frequently distributing it to their followers. I'm not suggesting they always speak the truth or that they're immune from criticism. Clearly, some of their views are false or not fully supported claims. But much of what they say is backed by research.

Pastors and evangelical commentators, by contrast, seem less knowledgeable and less willing to directly put forth the case for gender differences. They tend to admit or insist they exist, but they rarely discuss specifics, and when they do it's usually to highlight a counter-stereotypical and low-risk finding. They may bring up a study claiming that females make better orchestra conductors.[16] Or critique stereotypical male behavior of which they disapprove, such as an unwillingness to marry their girlfriends. Rarely do we encounter politically incorrect or risky material.[17]

The net result is that the online gurus come across as a much better source of truth than the church. What they say may not reflect God's moral truth, but they are far more effective in communicating practical, actionable information.

In a world where mainstream secular institutions are denying the realities of gender, where science can no longer define what a woman or a man is, the church needs to be the most trusted and reliable source of truth, not morally dubious online gurus. And this highlights the broader challenge for evangelicals in the negative world: we must learn how to convey the truth about what is real and important—such as gender complementarity—especially when there is solid evidentiary grounds for it. Minimally, this means having reliable access to data and statistics about marriage, divorce, and family life and then knowing how to use that information in a convincing and persuasive way.

THE REALITY OF ATTRACTION

Another gap between what evangelical leaders teach and what the secular men's gurus say is how we talk about the realities of attraction. Many of the online gurus frequently talk about attraction, while evangelical churches tend not to say much about it at all, preferring to emphasize attributes like men being a servant leader. Yet being a servant leader, while important, affects only one of the two major criteria that make a man a good marriage match: attraction and compatibility.

We all know attractive people who would be bad to date or marry. We also know wonderful people who might make a great spouse but to whom we're not attracted. And servant leadership falls under the compatibility heading. Christian women may want to marry a man who is godly, of good character, and wants to invest in his family and homelife, but that's not the only factor they're weighing. Just because a man is a high-quality servant leader doesn't mean Christian women will be attracted to him.

Evangelical megachurch pastor Matt Chandler says, "I keep saying it: Godliness is sexy to godly people."[18] But Jordan Peterson says, "Girls aren't attracted to boys who are their friends, even though they might like them, whatever that means. They are attracted to boys who win status contests with other boys."[19] So who's right? Or to put it another way, who's more accurate, more true to life and lived experience?

The Jordan Peterson quote helps us remember that women are attracted to characteristics like status and power,[20] confidence and charisma,[21] looks and style,[22] and resources like money. Conversely, as the OkCupid study we referenced earlier reminds us, men are attracted primarily to looks and youth in women. Other studies tell us that women prefer to marry "up," or at least not "down." This helps explain why their earning more college degrees than men creates challenges for college-educated Christian women looking for husbands.[23] They prefer not to marry a man who has no degree.

These dynamics are combining to create an effect most

people have seen, even if they can't quite articulate it—namely, when women are in their twenties, they hold most of the cards in relationships. But when they reach their thirties, men start to hold the cards. Such a great reversal has even been demonstrated through academic research on online dating.[24] This reality can lead to great unhappiness in older single women, which, as I mentioned earlier, might then be relayed to pastors who don't necessarily understand why this is true or know how best to address it.

Again, these examples highlight a broader truth—that evangelicals have to become better at giving people reliable information that equips them for the real world. We need to equip singles in our congregations how to maximize their chances of getting married and then having a successful marriage. And understanding the realities of how attraction and dating markets work today—how they actually work, not how we would like them to work—is an important part of that.

THE ROLE OF LAY EVANGELICALS

Notice how little most of what I've shared to this point has to do with the egalitarian versus complementarian debates about whether women can be pastors. What we're talking about isn't so much a theological issue to be studied and debated; it's basic, fundamental information about men and women and how they behave in today's relationship markets. Increasingly, information like this must be brought to bear in the context of biblical truth to address the challenges of life in the twenty-first century. If the church doesn't talk about this, people will look elsewhere for help.

But as I've already indicated, there's an obvious reason why most pastors don't talk about this—and perhaps shouldn't.

It's outside their area of expertise. Pastors are trained in the Bible and theology, not psychology, sociology, and data science. They may have picked up some practical knowledge from counseling, but they aren't dating coaches.

The church is more than its leaders. Evangelicals perhaps expect too much from pastors, who are expected to have the Christian answer to everything. But let's be honest. They're not equipped to provide this kind of relationship advice. In fact, it can be dangerous for them to try. The Bible doesn't lay out a clear model for dating relationships, for example, and approaches to dating vary widely across cultures. Dating is an extremely culture-bound activity. So when pastors venture into giving dating advice or seek to provide other forms of life-coaching apart from Scripture, they may inadvertently call the gospel into question if their advice turns out to be bad. Even if it's 100 percent right, sometimes the best advice can still produce bad results.

This is exemplified by the purity culture movement of the 1980s and '90s, which took biblical principles and then extrapolated them into well-intentioned but ultimately nonbiblical advice such as "kiss dating goodbye," backed with the apparent authority of Scripture. But it's not always possible to avoid an attempt to provide practical applications of Scripture that might have culture-bound components. So when Christians seek to apply the Bible in these ways, we must always be careful to show how we arrived at our conclusions, keeping the clear teaching of Scripture distinct from our culture-bound applications.

We also need to become less dependent on pastors for life applications by encouraging greater integration of laypeople's vocational expertise with Christian faith and practice. We need a generation of lay evangelicals who can convey information from within their own area of expertise but from a Christian metaphysical and moral point of view and with an eye toward pointing people to Christ. We need genuine

Christian psychology experts who can speak on the behavioral differences between the sexes just as authoritatively as Jordan Peterson does. Where evangelicals don't have expertise, people are instead turning to secular gurus who are better informed and unafraid to share their viewpoint.

This is one of my goals in this book. I'm seeking to bring my management consulting and journalistic skills to bear on some of the challenges facing the church today—not to replace pastoral or theological answers to those problems, but to hopefully complement what others are saying in those areas with insights derived from a different approach to a problem.

Another good example of this is Dave Ramsey and his approach to personal finances. Ramsey is an evangelical teacher and author, not a pastor or theologian, yet he provides financial advice informed by his evangelical perspective and beliefs. Some people criticize aspects of what he says and even does, but there's no doubt that he's helped a large number of people get out of debt and improve their financial position.

Living in the negative world, we need larger numbers of Christians who bring their expertise and wisdom into integration with their faith. We still need pastors and theologians and Bible scholars, of course, but we can't expect them to do this work alone, nor are they often equipped for it.

THE LIMITS OF EGALITARIANISM AND COMPLEMENTARIANISM

The topic of gender is also an example of where the negative world exposes the limits of prior world strategies. Egalitarianism was an outgrowth of second-wave feminism, a positive world phenomenon. Until recently, it was aligned with secular culture, making this the safer view to hold in secular society. But secular culture has now evolved, rejecting the gender binary entirely and denying that gender exists in any objective form. Secular society now denies things as basic as the biological reality of gender.

Having developed as a movement aligned with the secular vanguard, egalitarians will likely struggle not to accept these future evolutions as well. If they decline to embrace the new viewpoint that rejects a binary view of gender, they could find themselves in the new and uncomfortable position of holding a deeply unpopular position on gender and potentially being subject to significant cultural hostility.[25]

We see this happening, to some extent, with secular feminists who have rejected allowing transgendered male-to-female people into female domains. Several of them have been branded Trans-Exclusionary Radical Feminists, or TERFs. People holding to this view, like Harry Potter author J. K. Rowling, have been subjected to severe critiques.[26] Evangelical egalitarians may find their own positions are at odds with broader society and will have to accept being labeled as TERFs and all that comes with that in order to hold to their theological position. This is difficult for anyone, of course, but especially when you're used to being in sync with the culture on gender matters.

Complementarianism also faces its own existential challenges. Contrary to its claims, complementarianism is also a modern theological system. It was developed in the 1980s in response to currents reaching back to the 1970s. It was a reactive movement in response to feminist inroads into evangelical thought. Wayne Grudem, one of the principal architects of modern evangelical complementarianism, became interested in the topic through his Greek word studies on the meaning of the term *kephalē*, translated as "head" in Ephesians 5, but which feminist egalitarians argued instead meant "source," as in the headwaters of a river, and thus did not imply hierarchy.[27] The flagship organization Council on Biblical Manhood and Womanhood began with some meetings at the Evangelical Theological Society in the mid-1980s, leading to a formal theological statement in 1989 and a book outlining the views in 1991.[28]

Complementarianism rejected feminist egalitarianism, but it focused primarily on two key matters for which there seemed to be direct scriptural instruction: retaining the husband as the head of the home and a male-only pastorate.[29] Substantive complementarity was acknowledged but not articulated in detail. In *Recovering Biblical Manhood and Womanhood*, the key book expounding the complementarian system, John Piper defines masculinity this way:

> Here we take the definition of masculinity, a phrase at a time and unfold its meaning and implications.
>
> At the heart of mature masculinity is a sense of benevolent responsibility to lead, provide for and protect women in ways appropriate to a man's differing relationships . . . ["At the heart of"] signals that the definitions [for both mature masculinity and mature femininity] are not exhaustive. There is more to masculinity and femininity, but there is not less. We believe this is at the heart of what true manhood means, even if there is a mystery to our complementary existence that we will never exhaust.[30]

While masculinity extends beyond this definition, it's both clear and notable that Piper defines masculinity almost entirely in terms of men's relationship to women, dramatically limiting its scope. This seems to exclude the vast bulk of a man's life as being considered specifically masculine. Although Piper is perhaps the leading advocate of the thick complementarian system, his definition represents a significant thinning out of what it means to be uniquely a man.

The Danvers Statement, the complementarian confessional statement issued in 1987, also seemed to respond to feminist critiques of pre–sexual revolution gender roles related to male headship in the home by softening them, saying, "Husbands should forsake harsh or selfish leadership and grow in love and care for their wives."[31] This approach anticipates the development of the servant leader concept in which the role of the man in the home is conceived as primarily to serve his wife and children.

Sociologist James Davison Hunter saw this trend developing in real time. His 1987 book *Evangelicalism: The Coming Generation*, published the same year as the Danvers Statement, used strong words to describe the development of evangelical thought that was becoming complementarianism, labeling it "doublespeak." He wrote:

> An unusual kind of doublespeak is taking place. On the one hand, the man is encouraged to assert a forceful leadership in all matters pertaining to the organization and development of the family. This would include matters of spiritual maturation, child discipline, family responsibilities, and the myriad decisions any family has to make. He is to command respect and ultimately the willful submission of his wife and children. He is, after all, ultimately responsible for keeping his household in order. On the other hand, he is encouraged to cultivate the emotional development of his children and open and expressive emotional bonds of intimacy with both his children and his wife. The upshot is this: though the husband and father has ultimate authority, that authority is qualified by an emphasis on sentiment . . . In this sense, his authority becomes purely theoretical and abstract.
>
> . . .
>
> The emphasis on the requirement of the husband to love his wife . . . is so prominent that the relationship

remains hierarchical in principle only . . . By redefining
the husband's authority as an administrative technicality,
the marriage relationship as a functional equality, and her
nature as "weaker vessel" in exclusively physiological terms,
Evangelicals have been able to maintain the integrity of their
commitment to biblical literalism while at the same time
making the submission of women much less intellectually
and emotionally objectionable.[32]

Hunter identified three strands of evangelical thought
on gender from the 1950s forward. The first asserted what
might be called traditional gender roles, which unapologeti-
cally appealed to Scripture over culture in their defense. These
gender roles themselves were not timeless, but a product of the
midcentury era. Nevertheless, this first strand was an unapolo-
getic defense of the cultural status quo ante views on gender.
Hunter's third strand was feminist evangelicalism, which
became what we know today as egalitarianism.

The second strand, however, was a hybrid updating of
previous gender roles in response to what were agreed to be
legitimate feminist complaints. The second part of the previous quote is Hunter's description of this strand.[33] This is
clearly the strand that was developing into modern evangelical
complementarianism.

THE END OF TRIANGULATION

This deeper dive into the development of evangelical views on
gender is helpful for a more broad understanding of how various evangelicals approached changes in culture in the positive
and neutral world. Complementarianism was an early version
of what would later become known as a third way doctrine.

The terms "third way"—or alternatively, "triangulation"—became popular in association with the politics of President Bill Clinton and UK Labour leader and Prime Minister Tony Blair. These leaders attempted to synthesize certain aspects of both left and right politics into a hybrid centrist position that would be popular with voters. Clinton-Blair politics were developed in the neutral world era for Christianity. Perhaps unsurprisingly, third–way-ism became particularly associated in the evangelical world with the neutral world cultural engagement model.[34]

Complementarianism first developed in the positive world, but it, too, adopted a third way cultural engagement approach as it navigated the neutral world. It combined a conservative desire to maintain a male pastorate and men as the head of the home with feminist desires for access to other roles for women elsewhere. It also acknowledged concern about matters like abuse, including emotional abuse, which in the Danvers Statement was said to be undergoing an "upsurge." Additionally, the nature of men's role as head of the home was redefined to accommodate some feminist criticisms.

Yet just as Clinton and Blair's politics didn't last, third way approaches have also proven unstable. This is the case with complementarianism as it has navigated the neutral and now negative world, where a third way approach tends to win few adherents. Its thin complementarianism variant has become so thin that it seems likely to collapse into egalitarianism.

As pastor Kevin DeYoung said, "Sometimes complementarianism is, 'We're all the same except men have a list of one hundred things they can do, and women have a list of ninety-eight things they can do.' We just try to massage that. 'There's two things you can't do: you can't be the leader in the home and you can't be the leader in the church.' That is a complementarianism that seems destined to fail."[35]

The thick variant of complementarianism, by contrast, has received criticism from a growing number of conservatives who reject complementarianism as a third way compromise with feminism and instead offer a full-throated embrace of patriarchy. They are, in essence, resurrecting the pre-complementarian defense of pre–sexual revolution gender roles.

This neopatriarchy movement has grown increasingly popular in the negative world, where the emphasis is less about creating a language that must appeal to society at large. The very embrace of the term *patriarchy* shows a lack of concern with being accepted or approved of by society at large. Neopatriarchy rejects the mainstream consumer-friendly approach of seeker sensitivity or cultural engagement. Instead, it's designed to serve a subculture. To its credit, it has a missional component, seeking to reach those disaffected young men turning to secular men's gurus.

However, there are also substantive problems with this approach, namely the reality that contemporary America is not a patriarchy, nor can patriarchal views likely succeed in our modern egalitarian society. Patriarchy was always more than just a theological interpretation of Ephesians 5. It was a legal and cultural system in which the man of the house held real authority backed by the institutions of society. The Bible is patriarchal in many ways, but its cultural milieu was also patriarchal. The Roman *paterfamilias* held real, tangible power.

Today, America is a legally and culturally egalitarian society. Mainstream culture considers patriarchy illegitimate and if anything is hostile to husbands and fathers asserting authority. Among other things, divorce and child custody courts[36] and public assistance systems[37] undermine marriage and fathers, and even the church generally blames men for divorce.[38] A modern wife's ability to divorce her husband at any time for any reason, and generally to get at least an equitable if not a profitable settlement in the process, renders the notion of resurrecting patriarchy little more than playacting.

So a man is able to be a patriarch only as long as his wife wants to play along. If she changes her mind, the charade is over. Believing in or advocating for a revival of patriarchy today is somewhat like believing in the divine right of kings. We don't have a king in America. We also don't live in a patriarchy. Those who seek a return to patriarchy, like those with egalitarian and complementarian approaches, are also reacting to cultural change. We need to better understand why people gravitate toward each of these approaches, but none of them provide us with a clear road map to life in the negative world.

FACING THE CONDITIONS OF MODERNITY

Complementarianism and its conservative critics promoting a neopatriarchy have not grappled seriously with the changes in American culture resulting from the decline of Christianity post-1964 and the rise of modern ideologies. They have also failed to seriously grapple with the fundamental changes in the nature of the household wrought by industrialization.

The preindustrial world, which encompassed the vast bulk of human societies in history and the entire milieu of the Bible, was organized around productive households that were the center of economic production, education, elder care, health care, the social safety net, policing and defense, and community governance. Today, companies in the marketplace or the government provide virtually all those functions. And today's household is often mostly a source of companionship that also embraces the parts of the child-rearing process not outsourced to schools.

The fact that the household doesn't have as many functions today, or at least the same functions as it once did, is part of what has fragilized the family. In the past, families really needed each other, often as a matter of survival. Husbands and wives needed each other, and there was a real financial, emotional, and social dependence between them. People who were not part of a family household could suffer terribly. This is one reason the Bible shows a special concern for the widow and the orphan, who were isolated outside the household system.

Today, however, men and women can get along fairly well on their own, at least as a matter of meeting basic needs. If a marriage goes through a dip or a stressful episode, that might be all it takes for the couple to divorce, since life alone is not as difficult as it was several centuries ago.

The loss of the productive nature of the household also exposes a key weakness of both thick complementarianism and neopatriarchy. They have largely failed to articulate a compelling role for women apart from being mothers and housewives. Yet in the famous passage in Proverbs 31, the wife is at home but not simply keeping house. She's overseeing a large household commercial enterprise. And in the preindustrial household, women were at home, but they had a critical and economically productive role. They preserved and prepared food, spun the cloth and made the clothes, made soap and candles and more, and did everything that allowed their husbands time to tend the fields and build and repair their houses. Modern industrial society destroyed these old female roles, and conservative evangelicals tend to have a limited vision of what women can and should be doing today. Unsurprisingly, many women don't find the conservative evangelical vision of female vocation appealing, especially those with inclinations and talents beyond child-rearing.

Many other changes in the reality of marriage and family

life in the modern world must also be addressed—for example, the technological mediation of dating and marriage markets and how children went from being an asset to a cost center. These are just a few of the challenges we need to grapple with. Fortunately, however, progress is being made in several places.

One is the movement toward trying to recreate the productive household. We see this in the form of people pursuing rural homesteading[39] and home-based enterprises.[40] Another form of pursuing a productive household is "insourcing," or people beginning to do for themselves what they formerly paid others to do, ranging from home repairs to housecleaning. They're even educating their children at home. This overlaps with but is not coextensive with the neopatriarchy movement, and while this movement is subject to critique, recreating the productive household is one thing they got right.

Yet how possible it really is for the average household in an industrial society to be truly productive is an open question, perhaps without a good answer. But it's one of the questions we need to be asking. Making households functional as interdependent relational and cultural units is one way to strengthen the family and adapt to the negative world.

Complementarianism also got several things right when it stressed the concept of leadership. Some conservative critics of complementarianism have criticized the term *servant leadership* and challenged complementarians to use terms like *servant lordship* instead.[41] But today's husbands aren't lords— just as they aren't patriarchs. The word *leadership* accurately captures today's reality that husbands and fathers must operate in an influence model in a negative world culture. They can't just order people around and lead through power and positional authority.

This can be challenging for men, who often aren't as strong on emotional intelligence as women are. But it can be done and is necessary. The problem for many complementarians is that their model of intersexual dynamics is incomplete, limited, and in some places, just wrong. Consequently, their advice on how to exert influence in the home often fails, again leading men to turn to secular gurus or gravitate toward neo-patriarchy. Evangelical leaders need to do more work in taking the insights of biblical teaching and theological reflection and applying them in connection with the gender and intersexual dynamics of American culture—even if that truth isn't popular in secular society.

As we navigate this new world—a negative world in which Christian values, beliefs, and ethics aren't seen as good or helpful and are largely rejected—it's okay to acknowledge that this is a difficult time. The answers to what to do aren't obvious. But it's okay not to know all the answers, and sometimes we need to step back and ask if the answers we've assumed are still working today or if they're based on faulty assumptions. In the negative world, evangelical Christians need to be comfortable with unknowns and constant change. But even if we don't have all the answers, admitting what we don't know can be credentializing itself. And we can begin by finding the right areas where we need to look for the answers.

THE FUTURE OF GENDER THEOLOGY

It's a given that in the negative world, theological gender movements whose followers are unwilling to defy the secular consensus will ultimately submit to it. This is the fundamental challenge facing egalitarianism, and while the future is impossible to predict, current trends suggest that egalitarians will likely deform and ultimately embrace secular positions on gender and sexuality.

Theologies of triangulation are also likely to fail in the long run. As I previously mentioned, just as Clinton-Blair politics are out of favor today, so third way approaches in theology are losing their luster. This is the fundamental challenge facing complementarianism. And while it may be an attractive short-term option for some navigating the transition to the negative world, the reactionary approach of neopatriarchy seeks a return to a world that no longer exists—and likely can't coexist in any meaningful way in the contemporary American culture and legal environment.

In the past, evangelicals have sought to deftly navigate cultural change through a creative synthesis that attempts to affirm the biblical text while somehow affirming as much of secular trends as possible. But the negative world offers us an opportunity to step back from the fray and ask the most fundamental of questions: What is true? This is a biblical and theological question, yes, but it's also an anthropological, social-scientific, and economic question. It must take account of biblical truth but also what creation reveals about the general characteristics and behaviors of men and women as well as the realities of family life and the best environment for raising children (namely, in an intact family with their biological mother and father, assuming both are still living). It must reckon with the nature of industrial society and the conditions of modernity such as mass media and contemporary ideologies.

A great first attempt at this synthesis was produced in 1980 by Stephen B. Clark in his book *Man and Woman in Christ*. This is the book that Southern Baptist Theological Seminary president Al Mohler credits with converting him from an egalitarian to what would become complementarianism.[42] Unfortunately, evangelicals largely ignored Clark, perhaps because he's Catholic and his work fell into obscurity until it was recently republished. It remains, however, superior to any evangelical treatment, and while it requires updating, particularly in its survey of the scientific literature, it still makes a good starting point for today's thinkers.

Gender is one of the most critical areas for evangelicals to discern today, and as I noted in an earlier chapter, strengthening our own communities for the negative world requires that we repair our own sexual economy. We also have to provide the truth about how to make this repair to our own people, and there's a significant missional opportunity to pursue here. Although much of what he says is couched in elevated language, Jordan Peterson's advice is what in a previous era would have been called folk wisdom.[43] "Stand up straight with your shoulders back," one of his twelve rules, is the kind of advice boys used to get from their fathers or grandfathers. It's similar to sentiments like "Clean your room."

Yet Peterson has attracted millions of followers by being willing to say these kinds of things. The need is still there, particularly in areas like gender where many people are hurting. But by being a source of truth in an era when secular culture lies and creating a different, healthier community based on truth, the church can remain a light to the world—even if that world holds negative associations toward Christianity. In order for us to have church communities where marriage with children is the norm, divorce is the exception, perpetual singleness is only for those truly called to it by God, gender confusion must be addressed as well as pornography use and sex outside of marriage.

Gender is simply one area where the church needs to discern the truth and proclaim the truth, and I've highlighted it here not because it's the only area we need to focus on, but because it's critical to human flourishing. It's also a flashpoint area of cultural conflict where the world is promoting many lies and the evangelical church has been deficient in its teachings. It also illustrates the scale of the challenge evangelicals face today. Being a source of truth is not about repeating some preexisting slogans. It will require substantial resources and research to get it right.

The same is true of other areas like race and political engagement. Race is another flashpoint issue in the culture, and the church has clearly gotten it wrong in the past. Like gender and sexuality, it's also an area where secular approaches and ideologies are being imported wholesale into the church. Politics and political theology are also matters that require further work. Evangelicals have alternately been too political and also not active enough in developing political theory and political theology. They've tended to rely on Catholic scholars like Patrick Deneen to provide political diagnostics. And while Catholic perspectives can be a valuable resource for evangelicals to draw from, we can't outsource our thinking on politics or other matters to the Catholic Church.

Gender confusion, race relations, and politics are three of the biggest issues where the American evangelical church is presently in conflict with the culture. We have to be a source of truth in these areas as we engage our mission of communicating the ultimate truth of the gospel of Jesus Christ.

CHAPTER 12

BE PRUDENTIALLY ENGAGED

IN THE WAKE OF DONALD TRUMP'S PRESIDENCY, there's been much discussion about Christian—and specifically evangelical—support for Trump. Some support Trump himself, others claim to disapprove of the man but vote to support his policies, and still others believe he's evidence of a growing "Christian nationalism" that confuses Christian identity with national support and potentially racist agendas.[1] At the same time, others within evangelicalism are worried that churches are embracing secular academic views like critical race theory as the foundation for their activism on race.[2] The purpose of this book isn't to sort out all these issues, but these controversies raise important questions about the nature of political and social engagement in today's negative world.

America has a two-party political system, so voting almost always comes down to a choice between two candidates. And in the negative world, it's increasingly likely that both candidates will hold policy positions materially at odds with evangelical preferences. They may also both be, like Donald Trump and

Hillary Clinton, people of dubious or questionable moral character.[3] What should evangelicals do in these scenarios? How should they engage politically when both choices available are bad or at least morally compromised? How should evangelicals engage in broader society when many Christian beliefs are declared culturally illegitimate?

THE COUNSELS OF DISENGAGEMENT

An emerging and popular evangelical strategy is to respond to the negative world by withdrawing—taking a detached moral posture and not participating in political and cultural life. One focus of this approach is on keeping evangelical moral witness pure and unsullied by contact with unsavory characters like Trump. Christians and the church are to turn aside from corrupt partnership with this system to transform the world and instead focus on being salt and light through ministry such as caring for the poor.

But both sides of this coin are emphasized. As pastor Scott Sauls has said,

> Historically, Christians have most influenced society not as culture warriors but as a praying, worshiping, giving, neighbor-loving minority. If given the opportunity, would we return to that, or are partisanism and power now preferred as lord and savior?[4]

These sorts of arguments aren't always specific or clear as to what this kind of withdrawal from public life actually entails. They tend to emphasize more of a pietistic approach to the Christian life, but they convey the clear sentiment that culture war Christianity is bad and a de-politicized, de-engaged

Christianity is good. This view also seems ambivalent or even skeptical about Christians holding and using political or other forms of power. It's a form of countercultural Christianity influenced by an Anabaptist sensibility.

This form of apolitical Christianity was a hallmark of the neutral world cultural engagement approach, in which evangelicals were largely embedded in politically and culturally secular progressive milieux like big cities and college towns. It is reflected in the approach of sociologist James Davison Hunter's idea of "faithful presence," for example.[5] But with the transition to the negative world, it may be time to reexamine this approach. Those who promote it tend to also promote a cultural engagement or seeker sensitivity model. Since most evangelicals are Republican, it can also be viewed as an attempt to sever the link between evangelicalism and political conservativism in the public mind.

It's notable that social justice concerns that align with secular political left priorities today are rarely if ever included in the critiques of mixing Christianity with culture warring, politicking, or power. Those who argue this way rarely suggest that the church should turn away from social or political engagement on racial issues, for example.

THE PROBLEMS OF THE
CULTURE WAR MODEL

An element of this critique of the culture war approach is, however, helpful for us to consider. Some culture warriors have been too focused on politics and too closely identified with political conservatism in ways that have in some cases been exposed as hypocritical or partisan. This is evident in the different standards used to judge Donald Trump's fitness for leadership versus Bill Clinton's.

Writing in *National Affairs* in 2017, Alan Jacobs said, "One of the most surprising developments of the 2016 presidential campaign was the wholesale abandonment by many conservative Christians, including many Catholics and most evangelicals, of a position that they had once held almost unanimously: In politics, character counts."[6]

Because evangelicals in the case of Bill Clinton so heavily stressed the importance of upright character as a qualification for holding the office of president, there's no defense for evangelicals who fall back to making what they believe is the best choice between two bad options—supporting a candidate like Donald Trump. Any support looks like hypocrisy in the public's perception. On top of this, any number of evangelicals have gone beyond tolerating Trump as the best of two bad options to linking the Christian faith to him and Republican politics, on display, for example, at the Jericho March just after the 2020 election.[7]

The culture war model, as we've traditionally known it, has always had serious flaws as a model of relating to culture. In the negative world, it's especially obsolete. The overturning of *Roe v. Wade* may well prove to be the swan song for this approach and its attempt to influence society via politics. Although the overturning of this decision was an enormous political accomplishment, it takes place against a backdrop of near total defeat elsewhere in American culture.

The current skirmish line in the culture war seems to be whether transgendered male-to-female athletes should be allowed to compete in girls' sports. If that's where the fight is presently, one could arguably conclude that the culture war has already been lost.

But a world where secular society views Christianity negatively itself shows us that the culture war failed. We can't blame the culture warriors for causing a backlash against Christianity that brought about the negative world; these larger cultural shifts were heading in this direction for a long time. Yet we should still ask why this approach was unable to stop these changes—or even make much progress in slowing them down.

Ironically, the culture war movement itself may have hobbled the development and further maturing of evangelical political engagement. The simplistic view that Christians must vote Republican because Democrats support abortion[8] (a view still promoted) meant that as long as elected Republican officials promised to and did in fact appoint pro-life judges, they didn't have to do anything else to keep the evangelical vote.

Under this political logic, it's unsurprising that evangelicals have received little besides pro-life judges in recent decades, even though they've constituted the largest and most important voting bloc in the Republican party. As I noted in an earlier chapter, evangelicals have little influence or status in movement conservatism as well, and they are all but absent from the senior-most leadership positions at its think tanks and publications.

The inordinate focus on politics also led many culture war evangelicals to neglect other critical sources of power in our society. This includes the economic power of corporations, the intellectual power of universities, the cultural power of the media and entertainment companies, and the administrative domination of the permanent civil service bureaucracy. In his 2010 book *To Change the World*, sociologist James Davison Hunter, who had previously coined the term "culture war," demonstrated how evangelicals adopting a culture war approach in relating to the broader culture fundamentally misunderstood the nature of culture and how it changes.

Evangelicals have had a naive view of the economy as well, believing that corporations pursued profit maximization and so did not want to alienate potential customers by taking overtly partisan political stands. Yet today, not only do corporations not seek to maximize profit (but rather stock valuation),[9] they actively promote and serve as enforcers of the secular left social policy line. The culture warriors' *laissez-faire* approach to economics, taken from libertarian or classic liberal political theory and not the Bible or Protestant tradition, has left them ill-equipped to respond to this turn by corporate America.

TOWARD PRUDENTIAL ENGAGEMENT

I am neither a political scientist nor a political theologian. I have five years' experience working for a major conservative think tank, though, so I do know the conservative political world. But in what follows, I won't pretend to offer a detailed blueprint for exactly when and how evangelicals should engage in politics or attempt to change the culture in the negative world.

But as I said earlier, in the negative world, we're entering unknown territory. So much of my reason for writing *Life in the Negative World*, then, is to awaken concerned evangelicals to these changing cultural realities, to suggest we stop repeating the same mistakes with the same tired answers and approaches to relating to culture. As we recognize the challenges we face, the right actions will have to be developed. Some will work, some will fail, but we need to develop fresh strategies for the cultural realities we currently face.

Toward that end, I want to suggest one general principle in relation to evangelical political and social involvement as we move forward: *evangelicals must remain prudentially engaged.* While the negative world does call for a more countercultural approach, evangelicals should not withdraw from political or social engagement, as some advocate doing. We can't adopt a monastic approach in the hope that we will survive intact from the next season of cultural shifts in the Western world. Evangelicals paid a high price for neglecting or misunderstanding cultural and economic power, and there's no reason to believe that taking a hands-off approach to politics will produce better results than taking a hands-off approach to big business did.

Evangelicals might decide they aren't interested in politics, but politics will remain interested in them. If there's anything to be learned to this point in the negative world, it's that secular culture will not allow us to have a private faith. We will be confronted and asked to fall in line, and if we do not, we will face consequences.

The truth is politics matters to evangelicals. What happens in the political arena not only affects secular society but has a direct impact on us, our families, our churches, and our communities. Modern society no longer recognizes a distinction between the public and private spheres, a stance best summed up in the feminist slogan "the personal is political."[10] The government simply will not—does not—view any area of your life as potentially off-limits to its intrusions.[11]

Hence it is legitimate and important to vote, support candidates, run for office, challenge unjust and unconstitutional laws in court, promote good judicial nominees, and even exercise political power to promote the general welfare of the US population when there's an opportunity. In the negative world, evangelicals can still be elected to many offices and may even hold a significant share of positions in some states and localities. Those who do should take full advantage of that.

But while evangelicals should not abandon the field of politics, the shift to the negative world means that the culture war model needs to be reconsidered. This means shifting our efforts away from fighting cultural battles we're unlikely to win—or are unlikely to have lasting importance to some of the challenges I've already highlighted, such as repairing our own sexual economy and acquiring more ownership over our economic life. It means learning to navigate a world in which there may not be any great candidates to vote for as an evangelical Christian.

It also means being more strategic about which battles we choose to fight and what goals we seek to accomplish in the short-term, realizing that in the negative world there is neither institutional nor public support for much of what evangelicals might want to do. What should evangelicals do when the overturn of *Roe v. Wade* means decisions about the legality of abortion are returned to the states and yet a majority of voters in their state want abortion to be legal—at least on some level? This is where prudence, that is to say wisdom, has to come into play.

Prudential engagement also recognizes that not all evangelicals will come to the same conclusion about where and how to be involved politically and socially. We should be tolerant of evangelicals who make a different decision than we do in this matter. That doesn't mean we avoid political conversations or refrain from critical evaluations of other people's approaches. It's perfectly valid to say, as I just did, that the counsel advocating political disengagement should be rejected.

But we should respect those who hold views different from our own and seek to be attuned to them when they've honestly made a different decision. Given the complexities of differing backgrounds, experiences, and geographical contexts, we're unlikely as Christians to always agree on every issue. We must respect those who arrive at their convictions through a serious, bona fide, good-faith process of prudential judgment.

Part of updating toward a new evangelical approach to

politics in the negative world is to renegotiate the deal evangelicals have with political conservatism and the Republican
Party. Again, realistically, the US has only two political
parties—likely to remain true for the foreseeable future—so
in most cases being involved in politics in ways that matter
means choosing one of them. While some evangelicals will be
Democrats or at least vote for some Democratic candidates,[12]
most evangelicals will likely remain Republicans.

But again, the current deal, in which evangelicals vote
Republican but get nothing beyond pro-life judges, needs
to be renegotiated. Despite a growing post-Christian right,
Republicans simply can't win without evangelical votes, and
evangelicals should insist on getting more out of the deal than
they've been receiving—and to be clear, this does not equate
to pursuing a theocracy. It's entirely legitimate for Christian
voters to seek laws, policies, and political leaders who support
their values and way of life in ways that respect the rule of law
in a liberal democracy. And so it's entirely right for them to
expect that those they support should represent them on more
than a single issue, such as abortion.

But it's up to evangelicals to make this clear to those we
support. For example, a lot of evangelical money flows into
conservative think tanks that have few if any evangelical
senior leaders and are largely socially liberal in orientation.
Conservative evangelical donors should make it clear that their
continued funding of these organizations is contingent on their
being more responsive to evangelical concerns and hiring more
evangelical personnel.

Evangelicals also need to better understand how political
and social change takes place. In the past we've been weak or
overly simplistic in our assumptions about how change happens
in this country, which is why evangelicals embraced theories of
cultural change that were, as James Davison Hunter documents,

simply false. Some of this can be attributed to the failure of political conservatism, to which evangelicals outsourced much of their political thinking. Contrary to what some political conservatives seem to believe, not all the knowledge necessary to understand contemporary American economic, social, and political conditions and dynamics can be acquired by reading what we call the Great Books or by studying the Greco-Roman classics or the writings of the founders of the US, however valuable those sources might be.[13]

This also involves recognizing that what worked for secular activists won't always work for evangelicals. Studying the left's theories of cultural change or the behaviors of their activist groups is important, but those techniques can't naively be copied or transferred to the other side. Those methods are rooted in different power relations as well as different values and ethics. The means by which we effect change is innately connected to the final results we wish to see.

For example, evangelicals can't read Saul Alinksy's *Rules for Radicals* thinking it's possible to effect the change they want simply by doing what he did or suggests, although they may learn from it. Knowing how culture changes in general doesn't necessarily provide a road map for making change happen in alignment with evangelical goals and concerns. Change is context dependent, and the methods and means used shape the result.

For evangelicals to be successful in this, we'll need to develop competence and the qualifications necessary to assume culture-leading positions. These positions could be stepping into roles like a think tank president, a governorship or other elected office, or even a Supreme Court justice seat. To lead or govern well will require new skills and approaches to successfully adapt engagement strategies to a negative world, where a majority of people will disagree with many evangelical views.

Making prudential, wise decisions in these environments requires expertise and wisdom.

The key in all this is not to withdraw and isolate, whether an intentional withdrawal or the result of a culture war approach in which we are isolated and marginalized. To survive and thrive in the negative world, evangelicals must remain engaged in the world politically, socially, and culturally. There's no future in building a backwoods bubble or creating a community that's isolated.

There's also no avoiding the pressures of the negative world by being winsome enough. If you're authentically following Christ, the world will find something you say or do to critique, criticize, or cancel. Yet we can't abandon our calling to engage in evangelism and mission. We should seek to be salt and light through prudentially engaging in politics and culture, even in the negative world.

CONCLUSION

THE NEGATIVE WORLD POSES PROFOUND CHALLENGES to American evangelicals in the coming years. And a look at the long arc of secularization and the negative cultural and religious trends that have been ongoing for decades can easily create a profound sense of gloom and despair.

UC San Diego professor Edward Watts's book *The Final Pagan Generation* is about how Christianity conquered the Roman Empire, told from the standpoint of the last pre-Constantinian generation of pagans. They didn't understand what was happening to their world, or the full ramifications of Christianization and the actions of Constantine and his successors. Even the explicitly pro-pagan emperor Julian the Apostate was unable to reverse this course. Pagan civilization fell, and paganism went extinct a few centuries later.

Such books can make for uncomfortable reading. It's easy to start wondering, as Rod Dreher did in reviewing Watts's book, whether we might prove to be the last Christian generation in America.[1] French philosopher Chantal Delsol's talk of the end of the Christian world, referenced in chapter 3, can also make an evangelical feel depressed.

But those aren't the only stories that can or should be told. In AD 639, Islamic armies began their conquest of Christian Egypt, inaugurating a dark era for the Christians there. And yet, almost fourteen hundred years later, with Egypt still a Muslim country, around 5 to 10 percent of the people in Egypt today are still Christian. Today, with around a hundred million residents, that means as many as five to ten million Christians live there.[2] The estimated population of Egypt at the time of the Islamic conquest was only three to five million.[3] So there may be as many as twice as many Christians in Egypt today as there were at the end of its Roman Christian era.

Is everything wonderful for the largely Coptic Christians of Egypt? Of course not. They face ongoing persecution and challenges that Christians in America can't relate to.[4] But this fact remains: Christianity is still very much alive in Egypt.

The situation for American Christians is nowhere near as bad as what Egyptian Christians have experienced. There's no reason for us not to be optimistic about our future while still being realistic about the conditions we face. Evangelicals can survive and even thrive—even in the negative world of today's America. Christianity can have a bright future in this country.

We also don't know what God will or won't do. Multiple great awakenings have taken place in the American past.[5] The pendulum has swung between more socially liberal and socially conservative eras multiple times. History is never a straight line, and empires and regimes don't last forever. There is no inevitability to the direction the country has been taking. Profound "black swan" events often have dramatic and unforeseen consequences. And regardless of what our situation may look like, "nothing can hinder the LORD from saving, whether by many or by few" (1 Samuel 14:6).

But we can't be complacent either. The book of Ecclesiastes says there's a time for everything. A time to tear down and a time to build, a time to keep and a time to throw away, a time to be silent and a time to speak. With the transition to the negative world, we need to know what time it is.

Evangelicals can't expect that the strategies and structures of the positive and neutral worlds will continue to sustain us in this new era. This means more emphasis on being countercultural and less on relevance and transformation, though without completely abandoning them and indeed remaining focused on mission. Evangelicals have to at a minimum adapt what we're doing to new times and find new approaches as well. Finding strategies that work won't be easy or obvious, but we'll have to be comfortable with that uncertainty, be willing to try new things, and make adjustments as we see what works and what doesn't as the world changes around us.

I've attempted to provide some starter ideas by looking at the three critical dimensions of evangelical life: our personal and family lives, our churches and institutions, and evangelism and mission. Much of this likely includes several things we already knew we were supposed to be doing but probably weren't—at least not to the extent we need to. It goes without saying that we have to be obedient to God's Word. We have to build strong and stable families. We have to be a salt and light in the world.

But I've also identified some important areas that may have been less of a focus in the evangelical world. I hope you pay particular attention to them.

THE PURSUIT OF EXCELLENCE. Evangelicals need to become people with high levels of skill and competence in many fields, from the intellectual world to the law. We also need to value and approve of the desire for high-level achievement. A lack of high-level expertise has crippled evangelicalism in many ways, from embracing misguided theories of cultural change to being unable to assume the most key roles even within areas like political conservatism.

RESILIENCE AND ANTIFRAGILITY. With the increasing pressures of the negative world, evangelicals should be looking to structure households and institutions to be pressure resistant, or even to grow stronger from hostility.

ACQUIRING OWNERSHIP. Since mainstream institutions are increasingly hostile to Christian values, ownership of more of our own institutions, particularly businesses that can generate wealth and employ a significant number of people, is important.

SPEAKING TRUTH CLEARLY. The negative world's insistence on promoting unhealthy patterns of life and the absurd opens new opportunity for evangelism and mission through being willing to confidently and clearly speak truth. This requires that we adjust our own thinking in some key areas.

Again, these are general themes. How we apply them depends on our particular context. And they require us to think through what it means to apply them in our own lives.

Not everyone has the skills or personality for starting a business, but we can at least think about the kind of company we want to work for or the kind of career we want to pursue in light of the negative world. We might not have the financial resources to buy commercial real estate downtown, but we can think about intentionally choosing to live close to other people who are part of our church community. Most importantly, regardless of what we do in our own situations, we should be thinking in general about what we need to do differently in today's world.

Once more, *we have not been this way before.* And the answers and strategies of the past aren't guaranteed to work now, if they ever did. Evangelicals should not expect to find a simple formula to follow in exploring this new territory. If I succeed in what I hope to accomplish with this book, it won't be the last word but just the first of many put forth by people sharing what they've learned in finding flourishing in the negative world.

May the Lord guide us as we seek to faithfully follow him.

> Trust in the LORD with all your heart
> > and lean not on your own understanding;
> in all your ways submit to him,
> > and he will make your paths straight.
>
> —PROVERBS 3:5–6

NOTES

INTRODUCTION

1. My interview with the Benham Brothers.
2. Meredith Blake, "HGTV drops reality show starring anti-gay-marriage Christian activist," *Los Angeles Times*, May 8, 2014, https://www.baltimoresun.com/la-et-st-hgtv-drops-flip-it -forward-anti-gay-david-jason-benham-20140508-story.html; Jake Perlman, "HGTV Cancels 'Flip It Forward' Pilot amid Hosts' Anti-Gay Controversy," Entertainment, May 7, 2014, https://ew.com/article/2014/05/07/hgtv-cancels-pilot/.
3. "'Flip It Forward' Crew 'Blindsided'—HGTV Treated Us Like Dirt," TMZ, May 10, 2014, https://www.tmz.com/2014/05 /10/flip-it-forward-crew-david-jason-benham-tv-show-cancelled -hgtv.
4. Lauren Sandler, "Crossing a Divide, Seeking Good," *New York Times*, February 21, 2014, https://www.nytimes.com/2014 /02/23/movies/how-the-true-false-film-festival-and-a-church -work-together.html.
5. Dan Schindel, "After Anti-Trans Sermon, True/False Film Fest Divests from Its Church Partner," Hyperallergic, October 24, 2019, https://hyperallergic.com/524318/true-false-film-festival -crossing-church-anti-trans-sermon/.
6. Chris O'Falt, "The Unbridgeable Divide: How True/False's Celebrated Partnership with an Evangelical Church Imploded," Indie Wire, March 9, 2020, https://www.indiewire.com/2020

/03/true-false-film-fest-the-crossing-evangelical-church-partnership-1202215737/.

7. This is the RELTRAD, or religious tradition model. See Brian Steensland et al, "The Measure of American Religion: Toward Improving the State of the Art," *Social Forces* 9, no. 1 (September 2000), 291–318, https://academic.oup.com/sf/article/79/1/291/2233984.

8. Ashleigh Barraclough and Judd Boaz, "New Essendon CEO Andrew Thorburn steps down," ABC News, Australia, October 4, 2022, https://www.abc.net.au/news/2022-10-04/essendon-ceo-andrew-thorburn-church-homophobic-resigns/101499074.

CHAPTER 1: THE THREE WORLDS OF EVANGELICALISM

1. Carol Tucker, "The 1950s—Powerful Years for Religion," USCNews, June 16, 1997, https://news.usc.edu/25835/The-1950s-Powerful-Years-for-Religion/.

2. Address at the Freedoms Foundation, Waldorf-Astoria, New York City, New York, December 22, 1952, https://www.eisenhowerlibrary.gov/eisenhowers/quotes.

3. William I. Hitchcock, "How Dwight Eisenhower Found God in the White House," History, updated May 10, 2023, https://www.history.com/news/eisenhower-billy-graham-religion-in-god-we-trust.

4. See my retrospective on the WASP establishment: Aaron M. Renn, "Rediscovering E. Digby Baltzell's Sociology of Elites," *African Affairs* 5, no. 1 (spring 2021), https://americanaffairsjournal.org/2021/02/rediscovering-e-digby-baltzells-sociology-of-elites/.

5. Ayana Mathis, "What the Church Meant for James Baldwin," *New York Times Style Magazine*, December 4, 2020, https://www.nytimes.com/2020/12/04/t-magazine/james-baldwin-pentecostal-church.html.

6. Dr. Martin Luther King Jr., "Letter from Birmingham Jail" from April 16, 1963, Bill of Rights Institute, https://billofrightsinstitute.org/primary-sources/letter-from-birmingham-jail.

7. Russell Moore, "Is Christianity Dying?" May 12, 2015, https://www.russellmoore.com/2015/05/12/is-christianity-dying/.

8. This is a general statement describing primarily the environment of the major institutions of society. Actual conditions varied by place and domain. For example, in many rural areas, Christianity was and is still viewed as a positive.

9. Notwithstanding evangelical perceptions, even today there are faithful churches and many faithful Christians in the Episcopal Church.

10. James R. Dickenson and Paul Taylor, "Newspaper Stakeout Infuriates Hart," *Washington Post*, May 4, 1987, https://www.washingtonpost.com/wp-srv/local/longterm/tours/scandal/hart.htm.

11. Andrew Glass, "Drudge says Newsweek sitting on Lewinsky story, Jan. 17, 1998," Politico, January 17, 2013, https://www.politico.com/story/2013/01/this-day-in-politics-086305.

12. Jack Shafer, "Why Did NBC News Sit on the Trump Tape for So Long?" *Politico*, October 10, 2016, https://www.politico.com/magazine/story/2016/10/trump-tape-nbc-news-access-hollywood-billy-bush-214344/.

13. Robert B. Reich, "Secession of the Successful," *New York Times Magazine*, January 20, 1991, https://www.nytimes.com/1991/01/20/magazine/secession-of-the-successful.html.

14. There is significant debate around the meaning of the terms *woke* or *wokeness*, but I use roughly the Merriam-Webster definition of "politically liberal (as in matters of racial and social justice) especially in a way that is considered unreasonable or extreme."

15. Matthew Yglesias, "The Great Awokening," The Highlight by Vox, updated April 1, 2019, https://www.vox.com/2019/3/22/18259865/great-awokening-white-liberals-race-polling-trump-2020.

16. David Rozado, Musa Al-Gharbi, and Jamin Halberstadt, "Prevalence of Prejudice-Denoting Words in News Media Discourse: A Chronological Analysis," SAGE Journals, *Social*

Science Computer Review 41, no. 1, July 27, 2021, https://doi
.org/10.1177/08944393211031452.

17. Alex Tabarrok, "The NYTimes Is Woke," Marginal
    Revolution, June 2, 2019, https://marginalrevolution.com
    /marginalrevolution/2019/06/the-nytimes-is-woke.html.

18. Chris Cillizza and Sean Sullivan, "How Proposition 8
    passed in California—and why it wouldn't today," The
    Fix, the *Washington Post*, March 26, 2013, https://www
    .washingtonpost.com/news/the-fix/wp/2013/03/26/how
    -proposition-8-passed-in-california-and-why-it-wouldnt-today/.

19. Katy Steinmetz, "See Obama's 20-Year Evolution on LGBT
    Rights," *TIME*, April 10, 2015, https://time.com/3816952
    /obama-gay-lesbian-transgender-lgbt-rights/.

20. Paul Kengor, "Hillary Clinton's evolution on gay marriage:
    Column," *USA Today*, March 20, 2013, https://www.usatoday
    .com/story/opinion/2013/03/20/hillary-clinton-gay-marriage
    /2001229/.

21. Michael Lambert, "Donald Trump Waves LGBT Rainbow
    Flag at Colorado Rally," Advocate, October 31, 2016, https://
    www.advocate.com/2016/10/31/donald-trump-waves-lgbt
    -rainbow-flag-colorado-rally.

22. Jonathan Haidt (@JonHaidt), Twitter, March 7, 2022, https://
    twitter.com/JonHaidt/status/1500870465161764868.

23. Susan Donaldson James, "Pastor Warren Sets Inclusive Tone at
    Inaugural," ABC News, January 19, 2009, https://abcnews.go
    .com/Politics/Inauguration/rick-warren-invocation-president
    -obama-inauguration/story?id=6687731.

24. Sheryl Gay Stolberg, "Minister Backs Out of Speech at
    Inaugural," *New York Times*, January 10, 2013, https://www
    .nytimes.com/2013/01/11/us/politics/minister-withdraws-from
    -inaugural-program-after-controversy-over-comments-on-gay
    -rights.html.

25. Rod Dreher, *The Benedict Option: A Strategy for Christians in
    a Post-Christian Nation* (New York: Penguin Group Sentinel,
    reprint 2018).

26. "Lesslie Newbigin: Interview," interview by Andrew Walker, John Mark Ministries, January 9, 2003, https://www.jmm.org .au/articles/4.htm.

27. Charles Taylor, *A Secular Age* (Cambridge, MA: Harvard University Press, Belknap Press, reprint edition 2018).

28. Callum Brown, *The Death of Christian Britain: Understanding Secularization, 800–2000,* 2nd ed. (Abingdon, England: Routledge, 2008).

29. Geoffrey Kabaservice, *The Guardians: Kingman Brewster, His Circle, and the Rise of the Liberal Establishment* (New York: Harry Holt and Co., 2004), 15.

30. Michael Lipka, "5 Facts about the Pledge of Allegiance," Pew Research Center, September 4, 2013, https://www.pewresearch .org/fact-tank/2013/09/04/5-facts-about-the-pledge-of-allegiance/.

31. Andrew Glass, "'In God We Trust' to appear on all U.S. currency, July 11, 1955," Politico, July 11, 2017, https://www .politico.com/story/2017/07/11/in-god-we-trust-to-appear-on -all-us-currency-july-11-1955-240337.

32. "Federal Reserve Payments Study," Board of Governors of the Federal Reserve System, updated January 14, 2022, https:// www.federalreserve.gov/paymentsystems/december-2021 -findings-from-the-federal-reserve-payments-study.htm.

CHAPTER 2: STRATEGIES FOR THE POSITIVE AND NEUTRAL WORLDS

1. Brad Vermurlen, *Reformed Resurgence: The New Calvinist Movement and the Battle over American Evangelicalism* (New York: Oxford University Press, 2020).

2. James Davison Hunter, *To Change the World: The Irony, Tragedy & Possibility of Christianity in the Late Modern World* (New York: Oxford University Press, 2010).

3. The RELTRAD model noted previously.

4. Kevin Phillips, *Post-Conservative America: People, Politics, & Ideology in a Time of Crisis* (New York: Vintage Books, 1983), 46–48.

5. Phillips, *Post-Conservative America*, 90–91.

6. Jon Meacham, "The Editor's Desk," Newsweek, November 12, 2006, https://www.newsweek.com/editors-desk-106637.

7. James Davison Hunter, *American Evangelicalism: Conservative Religion and the Quandary of Modernity* (New Brunswick, NJ: Rutgers University Press, 1983).

8. Tom Gjelten, "2020 Faith Vote Reflects 2016 Patterns," NPR, November 3, 2020, https://www.npr.org/2020/11/08/932263516/2020-faith-vote-reflects-2016-patterns.

9. *The 700 Club* is the paradigmatic example here.

10. The church was founded in the suburb of Palatine, where it rented space in the Willow Creek Theater, see https://chicagoreader.com/news-politics/superchurch/.

11. The term is widely used to describe these churches, sometimes by critics of the model. See Dorothy Greco, "How the Seeker-Sensitive, Consumer Church Is Failing a Generation," *Christianity Today*, August 30, 2013, https://www.christianitytoday.com/ct/2013/august-web-only/how-seeker-sensitive-consumer-church-is-failing-generation.html.

12. Russell Chandler, "Column One: 'Customer' Poll Shapes a Church: A Minister Discovered Why People Don't Attend. He Founded One of the Nation's Most Successful Congregations," *Los Angeles Times*, December 11, 1989, https://www.latimes.com/archives/la-xpm-1989-12-11-mn-126-story.html.

13. Scot McKnight, "The Legacy of Willow Creek 3," *Christianity Today*, Jesus Creed, a blog by Scot McKnight, October 7, 2020, https://www.christianitytoday.com/scot-mcknight/2020/october/legacy-of-willow-creek-3.html.

14. "Two of the prototypes for the megachurch model—the original Calvary Chapel in Costa Mesa, California, and Willow Creek Community Church in South Barrington, Illinois—both trace their roots (albeit very differently) to the days of the Jesus People movement." Larry Eskridge, *God's Forever Family: The Jesus People Movement in America* (New York: Oxford University Press, 2013), 8.

15. See Kathy Keller, "Lessons Learned from 30 Years in Ministry," City to City, March 12, 2018, https://medium.com/redeemer -city-to-city/lessons-learned-from-30-years-in-ministry- e580d4afb846. In a reflection of thirty years of ministry at Redeemer Presbyterian Church, Kathy Keller describes how they eliminated evangelical specific language—"piousbabble" as she called it—as part of tuning Redeemer to be aligned with New York culture. She says, "We had to ask, 'Did it fit New York? Would people understand it? Would it get in the way of non-Christians hearing the gospel?' Those are the questions we asked of every single choice, starting back even with the naming of Redeemer." She even uses the term *seeker* to describe the type of person they initially drew.

16. Redeemer Presbyterian Church has a traditional liturgy.

17. Hillsong, which attracted celebrities like Justin Bieber, is an example of the hip-cool style. See Taffy Brodesser-Akner, "Inside Hillsong, the Church of Choice for Justin Bieber and Kevin Durant," *GQ*, December 17, 2015, https://www.gq.com /story/inside-hillsong-church-of-justin-bieber-kevin-durant.

18. A number of these churches describe themselves explicitly as "multi-ethnic," such as Mosaic Community Church in Seattle, https://seattle.mosaic.family/.

19. Some of these churches partner with or run arts organizations. The Crossing church, as noted in the Introduction, partnered with a local film festival and art gallery. Memorial Presbyterian Church in St. Louis hosts a nonprofit arts venue called The Chapel, http://www.memorialpca.org/chapel.html.

20. The "faith and work" movement is prominent in the urban church world, such as the VOCA Center or the Redeemer Center for Faith and Work in New York. This shows the emphasis on career.

21. The parachurch ministry Veritas Forum, which hosts serious intellectual discussions on college campuses, is an example of showing respect for the life of the mind. See https://www .veritas.org/.

22. Some prominent religion or reporters at major secular media outlets could themselves be classified as cultural engagement figures, such as Sarah Pulliam Bailey at the *Washington Post* or Alissa Wilkinson at Vox.

23. For example, Andy Crouch wrote a column strongly critical of Donald Trump. See Andy Crouch, "Speak Truth to Trump," Andy Crouch.com, originally appearing in *Christianity Today*, October 10, 2016, https://andy-crouch.com/articles/speak_truth_to_trump.

24. Bill Hybels's model, developed in response to market survey data, involved a degree of deliberate strategic choice.

25. H. Richard Niebuhr, *Christ and Culture* (New York: Harper & Row, 1975).

26. My account is an extremely brief synopsis of an extended analysis in Timothy Keller, *Center Church* (Grand Rapids: Zondervan, 2012), 194–237.

27. Keller, *Center Church*. Keller's account focuses primarily on Christian Reconstruction, a boutique movement outside the mainstream of the religious right.

28. Keller, *Center Church*, 197. Keller writes, "The Christian Right typically seeks cultural change through targeted political activism against abortion and same-sex marriage and for the promotion of the family and traditional values."

29. Keller, *Center Church*, 203. Keller writes, "More doctrinally orthodox leaders such as Rick Warren and Bill Hybels have deliberately sought to be explicit about sin and judgment. Nevertheless, churches that we could characterize as being in the seeker church movement still rather heavily rely on techniques of business, marketing, technology, and product development; have a strong emphasis on self-fulfillment and the practical benefits of faith to individuals; and use a language sometimes light on theological particulars."

30. Abraham Kuyper and neo-Calvinism were a major influence on Keller, and thus the many others Keller influenced are often influenced directly or indirectly by him as well. See

Collin Hansen's *Timothy Keller: His Spiritual and Intellectual Formation* (Grand Rapids: Zondervan, 2023).

31. One exception in size are theologically traditional Lutherans such as the Lutheran Church Missouri Synod, often classified as evangelical but culturally distinct from mainstream evangelicalism. They adhere to a Lutheran two kingdoms model. The New Monastics and neo-Anabaptists share certain sensibilities with the cultural engagement model, such an urban orientation (e.g., Shane Claiborne in inner city Philadelphia) and concern for social justice, but they are in many ways distinct as well.

32. The adherents of these groups may be more geographically dispersed, but the leadership and their sensibilities come from these three different geographic origins.

33. Only 37.9 percent of adults aged twenty-five and older in America have a bachelor's degree or higher. See Frances Alonzo, "Census Bureau Releases New Educational Attainment Data," United States Census Bureau, February 24, 2022, https://www.census.gov/newsroom/press-releases /2022/educational-attainment.html. And the Brookings Institution noted that among voters surveyed in 2016, "White evangelicals were less likely in the sample to report income over $150,000 and bachelor degree or higher education levels." See Jason Husser, "Why Trump is reliant on white evangelicals," April 6, 2020, Brookings, https://www.brookings.edu/blog/fixgov/2020/04/06/ why-trump-is-reliant-on-white-evangelicals/.

34. Seeker sensitivity and cultural engagement emerged in educated, affluent geographical locations like Orange County, California; northwest suburban Chicago; and Manhattan and were shaped by the demographics of those locations.

35. Peter Applebome, "Jerry Falwell, Moral Majority Founder, Dies at 73," *New York Times*, May 16, 2007, https://www .nytimes.com/2007/05/16/obituaries/16falwell.html.

36. See, for example, Tim Keller's explicit rejection of

fundamentalism in favor of a neo-evangelical sensibility in Timothy Keller, "The Decline and Renewal of the American Church (Extended Version)," Life in the Gospel, accessed June 1, 2023, https://quarterly.gospelinlife.com/decline-and-renewal-of-the-american-church-extended/.

37. See, for example, D. G. Hart, *The Lost Soul of American Protestantism* (Lanham, MD: Rowman & Littlefield).

38. Dan Morgan, "Falwell, Bakker and the Fundamentalists," *Washington Post*, March 29, 1987, https://www.washingtonpost.com/archive/opinions/1987/03/29/falwell-bakker-and-the-fundamentals/96b47785-22fa-48a5-801f-cdf69b792f3b/.

39. Liberty University does not appear to have been renamed for specifically anti-communist purposes, but the name does associate clearly with Americanism. The college was renamed in the runup to the national bicentennial, complete with a large replica of the Liberty Bell. See Sattler, Abigail Ruth, "Timeline and Important Dates of Liberty University" (2011), Faculty Publications and Presentations 52, https://digitalcommons.liberty.edu/lib_fac_pubs/52. Liberty University also built a 275-foot-tall "Freedom Tower." See Office of Communications & Public Engagement, "Topping off Freedom Tower: LU Celebrates Grand Opening of New Campus Landmark," Liberty University, February 5, 1018, https://www.liberty.edu/news/2018/02/05/topping-off-freedom-tower-lu-celebrates-grand-opening-of-new-campus-landmark/.

40. Francis Fukuyama, *The End of History and the Last Man,* Reissue Edition (New York: Free Press, 2006 [Originally published in 1992]).

41. Rod Dreher, *The Benedict Option: A Strategy for Christians in a Post-Christian Nation*, Reprint Edition (New York: Sentinel, 2018).

42. K. A. Ellis, "The Benedict Option's Blind Spots," *Christianity Today*, March 2, 2017, https://www.christianitytoday.com/ct/2017/february-web-only/benedict-options-blind-spots.html; Hannah Anderson, "The Benedict Option Isn't an Evangelical

Option," *Christianity Today*, March 2, 2017, https://www
.christianitytoday.com/ct/2017/february-web-only/benedict
-option-isnt-evangelical-option.html; John Inazu, "The
Benedict Option Falls Short of Real Pluralism," *Christianity
Today*, March 2, 2017, https://www.christianitytoday.com
/ct/2017/february-web-only/benedict-option-should-include
-muslims-too.html; David Fitch, "The Benedict Option's False
Dichotomy," *Christianity Today*, March 2, 2017, https://www
.christianitytoday.com/ct/2017/february-web-only/benedict
-options-false-dichotomy.html.

43. Peter Frank, "Makoto Fujimura: An Immanent Abstraction," *Los
Angeles Times*, accessed June 1, 2023, https://makotofujimura.com
/assets/pdf/An_Immanent_Abstraction.pdf.

44. David Brooks, "Looking for an Internet Cleanse," *New York
Times*, March 28, 2019, https://www.nytimes.com/2019/03/28
/opinion/internet-cleanse.html.

45. "Makoto Fujimura," Yale Center for Faith and Culture, accessed
June 2, 2023, https://faith.yale.edu/people/makoto-fujimura.

46. Kate Shellnutt, "Princeton Seminary Reforms Its Views
on Honoring Tim Keller," *Christianity Today*, March 22,
2017, https://www.christianitytoday.com/news/2017/march
/princeton-rescinds-tim-keller-kuyper-prize-women-ordination
.html.

47. Trillia Newbell, "Holistically Pro-Life," Ligonier, February 25,
2016, https://www.ligonier.org/learn/articles/holistically-pro
-life.

48. The *New York Times* noted that "Some pastors, however,
now either minimize their preaching on the subject or speak
of homosexuality in carefully contextualized sermons
emphasizing that everyone is a sinner and that Christians
should love and welcome all." Michael Paulson, "With Same-
Sex Decision, Evangelical Churches Address New Reality,"
New York Times, June 28, 2015, https://www.nytimes.com
/2015/06/29/us/with-same-sex-decision-evangelical-churches
-address-new-reality.html.

49. See, for example, the Revoice movement, https://www.revoice .org/about.

50. Eugene Scott, "Comparing Trump to Jesus, And Why Some Evangelicals Believe Trump Is God's Chosen One," *Washington Post*, December 18, 2019, https://www .washingtonpost.com/politics/2019/11/25/why-evangelicals -like-rick-perry-believe-that-trump-is-gods-chosen-one/.

51. Julia Duin, "The Christian Prophets Who Say Trump Is Coming Again," Politico, February 18, 2021, https://www .politico.com/news/magazine/2021/02/18/how-christian- prophets-give-credence-to-trumps-election-fantasies-469598.

52. See, for example, Duke Kwon and Greg Thompson, *Reparations: A Christian Call for Repentance and Renewal.*

53. Again, Tim Keller explicitly called for separation from fundamentalists and others he deemed too conservative. Tim Keller, "The Decline and Renewal of the American Church (Extended Version)," Life in the Gospel, accessed June 2, 2023, https://quarterly.gospelinlife.com/decline-and-renewal-of-the -american-church-extended/.

54. See, for example, David Brooks, "The Dissenters Trying to Save Evangelicalism from Itself," *New York Times*, February 4, 2022, https://www.nytimes.com/2022/02/04/opinion /evangelicalism-division-renewal.html.

55. For example, First Baptist Church Naples in Florida experienced severe controversies over wokeness and purported racism. See Patrick Riley, "Racism allegations rock First Baptist Church Naples after failed vote to affirm black pastor," *Naples Daily News*, November 8, 2019, https://www.naplesnews.com/story /news/local/2019/11/08/first-baptist-church-naples-vote-black -pastor-failed-due-racial-prejudice-led-failed-vote-black-past /4169277002/. There have also been controversies around the level of focus on race at Cru. See Curtis Yee, "Cru Divided Over Emphasis on Race," *Christianity Today*, June 3, 2021, https://www.christianitytoday.com/news/2021/june/cru-divided -over-emphasis-on-race.html.

56. As of 2023, French is a columnist for the *New York Times*.

57. Sean Illing, "The Trump presidency was a catastrophe for American Christianity," Vox, February 3, 2021, https://www.vox.com/22188646/trump-evangelical-christianity-david-french.

58. Providence Baptist Church on the Upper East Side of New York is an example.

59. See, for example, Carl Trueman, "The Failure of Evangelical Elites," *First Things*, November 2021, https://www.firstthings.com/article/2021/11/the-failure-of-evangelical-elites.

CHAPTER 3: STRATEGIES FOR THE NEGATIVE WORLD

1. Chantal Delsol, *La Fin de la Chrétienté* (New York: CERF, 2021).

2. Chantal Delsol, "The Return to Paganism," Kirk Center, July 5, 2022, https://kirkcenter.org/essays/the-return-to-paganism/.

3. Chantal Delsol, "The End of Christianity," Hungarian Conservative, December 29, 2021, https://www.hungarianconservative.com/articles/culture_society/the-end-of-christianity/.

4. For more on the development of management and administration, see Alfred D. Chandler Jr.'s *The Visible Hand: The Managerial Revolution in American Business* (Cambridge, MA: Belknap, 1993).

5. Patrick Deneen, "Moral Minority," *First Things*, April 2017, https://www.firstthings.com/article/2017/04/moral-minority.

6. John Fea, Laura Gifford, R. Marie Griffith, Lerone A. Martin, "Evangelicalism and Politics," The American Historian, accessed June 2, 2023, https://www.oah.org/tah/issues/2018/november/evangelicalism-and-politics/.

7. Aaron M. Renn, "Newsletter #53: Understanding the Dissident Right," June 15, 2021, https://aaronrenn.substack.com/p/newsletter-53-understanding-the-dissident.

8. Matthew Walther, "Rise of the Barstool conservatives," The Week, February 1, 2021, https://theweek.com/articles/964006/rise-barstool-conservatives.

9. "Kentucky voters reject constitutional amendment on

abortion," PBS, November 9, 2022, https://www.pbs.org /newshour/politics/kentucky-voters-reject-constitutional-amendment-on-abortion.

10. Keller, *Center Church*, 237–38.

11. Chad Vander Veen, "Crowdsourcing Helps Chicago Chamber of Commerce Find More Bus Riders," Government Technology, July 26, 2010, https://www.govtech.com/archive/crowdsourcing -helps-chicago-chamber-of-commerce.html.

CHAPTER 4: BECOME OBEDIENT

1. Timestaff, "Swimming Naked When the Tide Goes Out," Money, April 2, 2009, https://money.com/swimming-naked -when-the-tide-goes-out/.

2. From my modern English translation and adaptation of John Owen's *The Mortification of Sin* (Urbanophile, 2018).

3. Ryan P. Burge, "With Gen Z, Women Are No Longer More Religious than Men," *Christianity Today*, July 26, 2022, https://www.christianitytoday.com/news/2022/july/young -women-not-more-religious-than-men-gender-gap-gen-z.html.

4. Keller, "The Decline and Renewal of the American Church."

5. Edward Mote, "My Hope Is Built on Nothing Less," https:// library.timelesstruths.org/music/The_Solid_Rock/.

CHAPTER 5: BECOME EXCELLENT

1. Meredith Wadman, Jocelyn Kaiser, "NIH chief defends use of human fetal tissue as opponents decry it before congress," Science, December 13, 2018, https://www.science.org/content /article/nih-chief-defends-use-human-fetal-tissue-opponents -decry-it-congress.

2. For example, see Dr. Francis Collins, "From the NIH Director: NIH 2021 Pride Month," National Institutes of Health, June 4, 2021, https://www.edi.nih.gov/blog/news/nih-director-nih -2021-pride-month.

3. Dr. Timothy Keller, "The Decline and Renewal of the American Church: Part 4—the Strategy for Renewal," Life in

the Gospel, Summer 2022, https://quarterly.gospelinlife.com
/american-church-the-strategy-for-renewal/.

4. Keller, "The Decline and Renewal of the American Church:
Part 4—the Strategy for Renewal."

5. Institutions examined include the American Enterprise Institute,
Heritage Foundation, Manhattan Institute, Hudson Institute,
the Ethics and Public Policy Center, the Claremont Institute,
National Review, *City Journal*, *First Things*, *National Affairs*,
American Affairs, *The American Conservative*, and *The
Claremont Review of Books*. Rich Lowry, editor in chief of
National Review, is an evangelical. See Michael Cosper, "Rich
Lowry on Where Conservatism Goes from Here," *Christianity
Today*, November 17, 2020, https://www.christianitytoday.com
/ct/podcasts/cultivated/rich-lowry-on-where-conservatism-goes
-from-here.html.

6. I identified their religion via personal inquiry. As they have not
publicly disclosed their religious affiliation, I am not listing
their names here.

7. Aaron Renn, "Evangelicalism's Second-Class Status in
Conservatism," American Reformer, November 8, 2021,
https://americanreformer.org/2021/11/evangelicalisms-second
-class-status-in-conservatism/.

8. Megan Fowler, "Why Haven't There Been Any Evangelicals on
the Supreme Court?," *Christianity Today*, March 22, 2022,
https://www.christianitytoday.com/ct/2022/march-web-only
/supreme-court-justice-evangelical-protestant-catholic-nomin
.html.

9. Charles Taylor, *A Secular Age* (Cambridge, MA: Harvard
University Press, 2007).

10. Patrick J. Deneen, *Why Liberalism Failed* (New Haven, CT:
Yale University Press, 2018).

11. WPC Battleground, "The Three Worlds and the Tao: Joe
Rigney: Welcome to Negative World #2," YouTube, https://
www.youtube.com/watch?v=ukkQam7ZosM.

12. An apparent reference to William Wilberforce.

13. Wikipedia, s.v. "Tao," last edited June 6, 2023, https://en .wikipedia.org/wiki/Tao.

14. Harry Emerson Fosdick, *On Being a Real Person* (New York: HarperCollins, 1943).

15. Edouard I. Kolchinsky, Ulrich Kutschera, Uwe Hossfeld, Georgy S. Levit, "Russia's New Lysenkoism," Science Direct, July 4, 2017, https://www.sciencedirect.com/science/article/pii /S0960982217309491.

16. E. Digby Baltzell, *Philadelphia Gentlemen* (New Brunswick: Transaction Publishers, 1989, paperback edition), 224.

17. E. Digby Baltzell, *Puritan Boston and Quaker Philadelphia* (Boston: Beacon Press, 1982), 96–97.

18. Baltzell, *Philadelphia Gentlemen*, 225.

19. David A. Hollinger, "After Cloven Tongues of Fire: Ecumenical Protestantism and the Modern American Encounter with Diversity," *Journal of American History* (June 2011), https://academic.oup.com/jah/article-abstract/98/1/21 /873365?redirectedFrom=fulltext.

20. John D. Wilsey, *God's Cold Warrior: The Life and Faith of John Foster Dulles* (Grand Rapids: Eerdmans, 2021), 197.

21. Adam Omelianchuk, "Why Do Evangelicals Convert to Catholicism?" *First Things*, March 25, 2010, https://www .firstthings.com/blogs/firstthoughts/2010/03/why-do -evangelicals-convert-to-catholicism.

22. Tyler Cowen, *Average Is Over: Powering America Beyond the Age of Great Stagnation* (New York: Plume, 2014).

CHAPTER 6: BECOME RESILIENT

1. Jon Ronson, "How One Stupid Tweet Blew Up Justine Sacco's Life," *New York Times Magazine,* February 12, 2015, https:// www.nytimes.com/2015/02/15/magazine/how-one-stupid -tweet-ruined-justine-saccos-life.html.

2. Nico Grant, Ian King, "Cisco Fires Workers for Racial Comments During Diversity Forum," Yahoo Finance, July 17, 2020, https://finance.yahoo.com/news/cisco-fires-workers -racial-comments-100000113.html.

3. "Hateful Conduct," Twitter, accessed June 3, 2023, https://help.twitter.com/en/rules-and-policies/hateful-conduct-policy.

4. Marina Pitofsky, "Twitter suspends GOP lawmaker Jim Banks' official account for misgendering four-star officer," *USA Today*, October 25, 2021, https://www.usatoday.com/story/news/politics/2021/10/25/rep-jim-banks-suspended-twitter-misgendering-transgender-official/8541515002/.

5. "84% Say Americans being Afraid to Exercise Freedom of Speech is a Serious Problem," Sienna College Research Institute, March 21, 2022, https://scri.siena.edu/2022/03/21/84-say-americans-being-afraid-to-exercisefreedom-of-speech-is-a-serious-problem/.

6. Nassim Taleb, *The Black Swan: The Impact of the Highly Improbable,* Incerto (New York: Random House, 2007).

7. Reuters, "Put Fannie, Freddie into Federal Receivership: WSJ," CNBC, July 15, 2008, https://www.cnbc.com/2008/07/15/put-fannie-freddie-into-federal-receivership-wsj.html.

8. The books are *Fooled by Randomness*, *The Black Swan*, *Antifragile*, a book of aphorisms called *The Bed of Procrustes*, and *Skin in the Game*.

9. Thomas J. Stanley and William D. Danko, *The Millionaire Next Door: The Surprising Secrets of America's Wealthy* (New York: Gallery, 1996).

10. Technically a major terrorist attack could be a "gray swan" because it's a rare event, but one we could conceive of happening.

11. Dan Zak, "'Nothing ever ends': Sorting through Rumsfeld's knowns and unknowns," *Washington Post*, July 1, 2021, https://www.washingtonpost.com/lifestyle/style/rumsfeld-dead-words-known-unknowns/2021/07/01/831175c2-d9df-11eb-bb9e-70fda8c37057_story.html.

12. Nassim Taleb, *Antifragile: Things That Gain from Disorder*, Incerto (New York: Random House, 2014).

13. Nick Bascom, "Probing Question: Why Did Mammals Survive the 'K/T Extinction'?" Penn State University, January 18, 2010, https://www.psu.edu/news/research/story/probing-question-why-did-mammals-survive-k-t-extinction/.

14. Taleb, *Antifragile*.

15. Sandi Doughton, "Mars Hill Celebrates New Home in Historic Downtown Church," *Seattle Times*, January 13, 2013, https://www.seattletimes.com/seattle-news/mars-hill-celebrates-new-home-in-historic-downtown-church/.

16. John O'Brien, "Mars Hill Church Disbands After Mark Driscoll's Resignation," NPR, November 1, 2014, https://kuow.org/stories/mars-hill-church-disbands-after-mark-driscolls-resignation/.

17. See Ramsey's Financial Peace University, https://www.ramseysolutions.com/ramseyplus/financial-peace.

18. https://www.mrmoneymustache.com/.

19. Steven Kurutz, "How to Retire in Your 30s With $1 Million in the Bank," the *New York Times*, September 1, 2018, https://www.nytimes.com/2018/09/01/style/fire-financial-independence-retire-early.html.

20. Taleb, *Antifragile*.

21. John Piper, "Boasting Only in the Cross," Desiring God, May 20, 2000, https://www.desiringgod.org/messages/boasting-only-in-the-cross.

22. The Bubp family story is from an interview with Ken Bubp.

23. Interview with Ken Bubp.

24. According to one survey, 56 percent of Americans don't have enough money to cover an unexpected $1,000 expense. Having even a small amount of savings for these contingencies can be beneficial to households of modest incomes, independent of negative world specific considerations. See Carmen Reinicke, "56% of Americans Can't Cover a $1,000 Emergency Expense with Savings," CNBC, January 19, 2022, https://www.cnbc.com/2022/01/19/56percent-of-americans-cant-cover-a-1000-emergency-expense-with-savings.html.

25. Barna, "38% of U.S. Pastors Have Thought About Quitting Full-Time Ministry in the Past Year," Barna, November 16, 2021, https://www.barna.com/research/pastors-well-being/.

26. Barna, "38% of U.S. Pastors."

27. Michelle Boorstein, "The First Christmas as a Layperson:

Burned Out by the Pandemic, Many Clergy Quit in the Past Year," *Washington Post*, December 24, 2021, https://www.washingtonpost.com/religion/2021/12/24/christmas-covid-pandemic-clergy-quit/.

28. Jean Hopfensperger, "Minneapolis Megachurch Loses 3 Pastors amid 'Painful and Confusing Moment,'" *Star Tribune*, August 14, 2021, https://www.startribune.com/3-pastors-leave-bethlehem-baptist-church-one-citing-toxic-culture/600087938/.

29. "Letter to Congregation from Abe Cho," Eastside Redeemer, April 26, 2021, https://eastside.redeemer.com/assets/uploads/2021-04-26-letters-from-abe-and-the-session.pdf.

30. Allyson Chiu, "'My Aim Was in No Way to Endorse the President': Pastor Explains Why He Prayed for Trump," *Washington Post*, June 4, 2019, https://www.washingtonpost.com/nation/2019/06/04/my-aim-was-no-way-endorse-president-pastor-explains-why-he-prayed-trump/.

31. Bob Smietana, "David Platt's Dreams for McLean Bible Church Sour Members File Lawsuit over Elder Vote," Religion News Service, July 20, 2021, https://religionnews.com/2021/07/20/david-platt-mclean-bible-lawsuit-crt-woke-liberal-radical-votes-lawsuit/.

32. Elliot Grudem, "Pastors Need Friends Too," Desiring God, February 10, 2018, https://www.desiringgod.org/articles/pastors-need-friends-too.

33. Kristen Plinke Bentley, "Stability Amidst Turbulent Times: the Benefits of Bi-Vocational Ministry," The Association of Theological Schools, May 2019, https://www.ats.edu/files/galleries/stability-amidst-turbulent-times-the-benefits-of-bi-vocational-ministry.pdf.

34. Interview with C. R. Wiley.

CHAPTER 7: PURSUE INSTITUTIONAL INTEGRITY

1. Jeffrey M. Jones, "Confidence in U.S. Institutions Down; Average at New Low," Gallup, July 5, 2022, https://news

.gallup.com/poll/394283/confidence-institutions-down-average
-new-low.aspx.

2. See the 2022 SBC report on sexual abuse, for example,
"Guidepost Solutions' Report of the Independent Investigation,"
SBC, May 2022, https://www.sataskforce.net/updates/guidepost
-solutions-report-of-the-independent-investigation.

3. Sara Nathan, Mara Siegler, "Carl Lentz's 'Multiple' Affairs
Allegedly Known to Hillsong for Years," Page Six, December
4, 2020, https://pagesix.com/2020/12/04/carl-lentzs-multiple
-affairs-allegedly-known-to-hillsong/.

4. Stephen Baskerville, "The Ways in Which Colleges Legally
Silence Troublesome Scholars," The James G. Martin Center for
Academic Renewal, January 6, 2021, https://www.jamesgmartin
.center/2021/01/the-ways-in-which-colleges-legally-silence
-troublesome-scholars/.

5. Liberty University is an example of an institution that allegedly
used non-disclosure agreements to silence would-be critics. See
Michael Poliakoff, "What Liberty University Tells Us about
Derelict Trustees," Forbes, November 7, 2019, https://www
.forbes.com/sites/michaelpoliakoff/2019/11/07/what-liberty
-university-tells-us-about-derelict-trustees/.

6. Michael Brice-Saddler, "A Wealthy Televangelist Explains His
Fleet of Private Jets: 'It's a Biblical Thing,'" *Washington Post*,
June 3, 2019, https://www.washingtonpost.com/religion/2019
/06/04/wealthy-televangelist-explains-his-fleet-private-jets-its
-biblical-thing/.

7. Much of the original criticism of MacDonald arose on an
anonymously published blog called "The Elephant Debt," a play
on MacDonald's controversial Elephant Room debate series.

8. The National Partnership in the Presbyterian Church in
America is an example. See Brad Isbell, "Smells Like Party
Spirit," Reformation 21, November 4, 2021, https://www
.reformation21.org/blog/smells-like-party-spirit.

9. It is important to note that there are still many faithful
mainline congregations, but the denominations institutionally

have largely departed from a gospel focus as evangelicals would understand it.

10. Brian Armstrong, "Coinbase Is a Mission Focused Company," Coinbase, September 27, 2020, https://www.coinbase.com /blog/coinbase-is-a-mission-focused-company.

11. Michael McSweeney, "Coinbase CEO Says 'about 5% of Employees' Have Taken Severance Packages after Controversial 'Mission' Post," October 8, 2020, https://www.theblock.co /linked/80230/coinbase-ceo-60-employees-severance-exits.

12. "'Tokenized': Inside Black Workers' Struggles at the King of Crypto Start Ups," *New York Times*, November 27, 2020, https://www.nytimes.com/2020/11/27/technology/coinbase -cryptocurrency-black-employees.html.

13. "Cryptocurrency Start-Up Underpaid Women and Black Employees, Data Shows," *New York Times*, December 29, 2020, https://www.nytimes.com/2020/12/29/technology /coinbase-pay-employees.html; "Tokenized," *New York Times*.

14. Basecamp is a small but influential company whose founders have written several books and produced an important open source technology framework. See Casey Newton, "Inside the All-Hands Meeting That Led to a Third of Basecamp Employees Quitting," The Verge, May 3, 2021, https://www .theverge.com/2021/5/3/22418208/basecamp-all-hands -meeting-employee-resignations-buyouts-implosion.

15. "Sustainable Investing at BlackRock," accessed June 3, 2023, https://www.blackrock.com/ch/individual/en/themes /sustainable-investing.

16. Peter Wehner, "The Evangelical Church Is Breaking Apart," *Atlantic*, October 24, 2021, https://www.theatlantic.com /ideas/archive/2021/10/evangelical-trump-christians-politics /620469/.

17. Tim Keller, "The Decline and Renewal of the American Church," Life in the Gospel, accessed June 3, 2023, https://quarterly .gospelinlife.com/decline-and-renewal-of-the-american-church -extended/; I again wish to note that there are many faithful

Christians in churches that are part of mainline denominations. The problems they've experienced are not universal.

18. Tim Keller, "Why Plant Church?," Redeemer City to City, January 1, 2002, https://redeemercitytocity.com/articles-stories /why-plant-churches.

19. Adam Gabbatt, "Losing Their Religion: Why Us Churches Are on the Decline," *Guardian*, January 22, 2023, https://www .theguardian.com/us-news/2023/jan/22/us-churches-closing -religion-covid-christianity.

20. "The Church with the $6 Billion Portfolio," *New York Times*, February 8, 2019, https://www.nytimes.com/2019/02/08 /nyregion/trinity-church-manhattan-real-estate.html.

21. On projected enrollment declines, see Nathan D. Grawe, *Demographics and the Demand for Higher Education* (Baltimore: Johns Hopkins University Press, 2018).

CHAPTER 8: PURSUE COMMUNITY STRENGTH

1. Education pioneer Horace Mann said that the school system "earnestly inculcates all Christian morals." See David Carleton, "Horace Mann," The First Amendment Encyclopedia, accessed June 4, 2023, https://www.mtsu.edu/first-amendment/article /1283/horace-mann.

2. Hana M. Ryman, J. Mark Alcorn, "Prayer in Public Schools," The First Amendment Encyclopedia, accessed June 4, 2023, https://www.mtsu.edu/first-amendment/article/1518/prayer-in -public-schools.

3. For example, many schools do not inform parents of information regarding a child's gender transition. See Donna St. George, "Gender Transitions at School Spur Debate over When, or If, Parents Are Told," *Washington Post*, July 18, 2022, https://www.washingtonpost.com/education/2022/07/18 /gender-transition-school-parent-notification/.

4. "What Are the Scout Oath and Scout Law?" Boy Scouts of America, accessed June 4, 2023, https://www.scouting.org /about/faq/question10/.

5. Robert Peterson, ed., "The Beginnings of a Partnership," *Scouting Magazine*, May–June 2004, https://scoutingmagazine .org/issues/0405/d-wwas.html.

6. Camila Domonoske, "Boy Scouts Changing Name To 'Scouts BSA,' As Girls Welcomed into Program," NPR, May 2, 2018, https://www.npr.org/sections/thetwo-way/2018/05/02 /607678097/boy-scouts-changing-name-to-scouts-bsa-as-girls -welcomed-into-program.

7. These include Harvard, Yale, and Princeton. See Dr. Roger Schultz, "Christianity and the American University," Liberty Journal, February 26, 2019, https://www.liberty.edu/journal /article/christianity-and-the-american-university/.

8. Maya Yang, "Harvard University's New Chief Chaplain Is ... an Atheist," *Guardian*, August 28, 2021, https://www .theguardian.com/education/2021/aug/28/harvard-university -chief-chaplain-atheist.

9. See Jake Meador's critique, "The Three Ages of Christian American Exceptionalism," Mere Orthodoxy, May 31, 2022, https://mereorthodoxy.com/christian-nationalism/.

10. Studies of Muslims show different effects for their experience of racial versus religions discrimination, illustrating the difference between the two. See, for example, Zahra Murtaza, "The Impact of Concurrent Racial and Religious Discrimination on the Mental Health and Well-Being of Muslim Young Adults," PhD diss. (Georgia State University, 2020).

11. While the majority of black Americans are Christian, a visible minority are Muslim, including multiple black members of Congress such as Andre Carson and former Congressman Keith Ellison. See "African American Muslims," Harvard Divinity School, accessed June 4, 2023, https://rpl.hds.harvard.edu/religion -context/case-studies/minority-america/african-american-muslims.

12. Christians in total, including not just evangelicals but also Catholics, Mainline Protestants, and Black Protestants, are down to 64 percent of the US population and trending toward minority status. See "Modeling the Future of Religion in

America," Pew Research, September 13, 2022, https://www
.pewresearch.org/religion/2022/09/13/modeling-the-future-of
-religion-in-america/.

13. This was the overlooked core message of Rod Dreher's book
Benedict Option. Andy Crouch observed that 80 percent of the
book was about the claim that "due to a lack of meaningful
discipleship and accommodation to various features of
secularized modernity and consumer culture, the collapse of
Christian belief and practice is likely among members of the
dominant culture (and many minority cultures) in the United
States within a generation or so," but that only about 10
percent of the media coverage of the book discussed this and
only 2 percent of the social media debate discussed it. Crouch
rates this claim as 90 percent likely to be true. See "The
Benedict Option in Percentanges," Andy Crouch, accessed June
4, 2023, https://andy-crouch.com/extras/the_benedict_option
_in_percentages.

14. They are also religions that overlap with ethnicity.

15. For example, Americans typically think of "Hispanic" as an
ethnic category, but it comprises many distinct nationalities
and ethnicities that don't always identify with each other and
are often in conflict. For example, there's long been conflict
between Mexican and Puerto Rican communities in the United
States. See Alan Feuer, "Little but Language in Common;
Mexicans and Puerto Ricans Quarrel in East Harlem,"
New York Times, September 6, 2003, https://www.nytimes
.com/2003/09/06/nyregion/little-but-language-in-common
-mexicans-and-puerto-ricans-quarrel-in-east-harlem.html.
At the same time, there are pan-Hispanic organizations like
various Hispanic chambers of commerce.

16. Julius Krein, "James Burnham's Managerial Elite," *American
Affairs Journal*, September 2017, https://americanaffairsjournal
.org/2017/02/james-burnhams-managerial-elite/.

17. For example, John O'Sullivan noted that a post-Christian
society is "rooted in the history, culture, and practices of

Christianity but in which the religious beliefs of Christianity have been either rejected or, worse, forgotten." See John O'Sullivan, "Our Post-Christian Society," *National Review*, December 14, 2013, https://www.nationalreview.com/2013/12 /our-post-christian-society-john-osullivan/.

18. For example, sociologist E. Digby Baltzell, whom I discussed in chapter 5.

19. This can be seen in things ranging from Notre Dame's highly patriotic football pre-game rituals to Senator Joseph McCarthy's staunch anti-communist crusading.

20. Complaints that formerly Christian institutions like Ivy League schools have forgotten their Christians roots go back at least to William F. Buckley's 1951 *God and Man at Yale* (Washington, DC: Henry Regnery Company, 1951).

21. Among the indicators of demographic health, Utah is the youngest state in America. See Lindsay Whitehurst, "Utah's Breakneck Growth Kept It the Youngest State in U.S.," AP News, August 12, 2021, https://apnews.com /article/health-coronavirus-pandemic-utah-census-2020 -b79965e391b1d5aebc2060fac52bdb9c. It also has the highest average household size. See https://worldpopulationreview .com/state-rankings/average-household-size-by-state.

22. Jennifer Toomer-Cook, "So Few LDS Schools," Deseret News, November 30, 2003, https://www.deseret.com/2003/11/30 /19798734/so-few-lds-schools.

23. Gary Fields, Brady McCombs, "We Didn't Leave Boy Scouts, They Left Us, Says Latter-Day Saint Apostle," *The Salt Lake City Tribune,* November 15, 2019, https://www.sltrib.com /religion/2019/11/15/lds-church-leader-we/.

24. Aaron M. Renn, "Classical Christian Education and the Christian Higher Education Gap," AR, March 23, 2023, https:// aaronrenn.substack.com/p/classical-christian-education-and.

25. During the COVID-19 pandemic, the national homeschooling rate reached 11.1 percent. Not all homeschoolers are Christian, but many are. See Casey Eggleston, Jason Fields, "Census

Bureau's Household Pulse Survey Shows Significant Increase in Homeschooling Rates in Fall 2020," United States Census Bureau, March 22, 2021, https://www.census.gov/library /stories/2021/03/homeschooling-on-the-rise-during-covid-19 -pandemic.html.

26. "Christian Schools Boom in a Revolt against Curriculum and Pandemic Rules," *New York Times*, October 19, 2021, https:// www.nytimes.com/2021/10/19/us/christian-schools-growth .html.

27. Diane Ravitch, "White Evangelicals Want to Destroy the Public Schools," Diane Ravitch's blog, July 22, 2021, https:// dianeravitch.net/2021/07/22/white-evangelicals-want-to -destroy-the-public-schools/.

28. Robert P. Lockwood, "Anti-Catholicism and the History of Catholic School Funding," Catholic League, February 2002, https://www.catholicleague.org/anti-catholicism-and-the -history-of-catholic-school-funding/.

29. For example, the extensive, long-term closures of schools during the pandemic is now widely viewed as a mistake with severe consequences for children's education. See Derek Thompson, "School Closures Were a Failed Policy," *Atlantic*, October 26, 2022, https://www.theatlantic.com/newsletters /archive/2022/10/pandemic-school-closures-americas-learning -loss/671868/.

30. Andy Crouch, "What's So Great About 'The Common Good'?," *Christianity Today*, October 12, 2012, https://www .christianitytoday.com/ct/2012/november/whats-so-great-about -common-good.html.

31. See, for example, Andrew O'Hehir, "Why My Kids Are Pop-Culture Illiterate," Salon, August 29, 2010, https://www.salon .com/2010/08/29/homeschooling_dora_the_explorer/.

32. Joy C. Ashford, "Twenty One Pilots' Evangelical Gamble," The Harvard Crimson, December 11, 2018, https://www .thecrimson.com/article/2018/12/11/twenty-one-pilots -evangelical-gamble/.

33. Terry Teachout, "The Common Culture, R.I.P.," The Washington Examiner, October 13, 1997, https://www .washingtonexaminer.com/weekly-standard/the-common -culture-r-i-p.

34. Bruce Springsteen, "57 Channels (And Nothin' On)," Spotify, https://open.spotify.com/track/42eWzCqHuCD5QRwzq3I24e.

35. Chris Bumbaca, "NFL Says 'Football Is Gay' in New Commercial That Makes Clear Its Support of LGBTQ+ Community," USA Today, June 28, 2021, https://www .usatoday.com/story/sports/nfl/2021/06/28/nfl-carl-nassib -football-gay-commercial/7783421002/.

36. Reece Rogers, "How Electronic Arts Tries to Make Diverse Video Games," Wired, July 25, 2022, https://www.wired.com /story/electronic-arts-inclusive-diverse-video-games/.

37. In the business world, these often go under rubrics like ESG (environmental, social, and governance goals) and DEI (diversity, equity, and inclusion).

38. See, for example, Walter Lippman's *Public Opinion: How People Decide; The Role of News, Propaganda and Manufactures Consent in Modern Democracy and Political Elections* (Blacksburg, VA: Wilder, 2010, originally published in 1922) and Edward Herman and Noam Chomsky's *Manufacturing Consent* (New York: Pantheon, 1988, 2002).

39. A term sociologists Christian Smith and Melissa Lundquist Denton coined to describe the beliefs of American teenagers. They believe God exists, wants them to be good and nice, and wants them to be happy, but is not particularly involved in their lives unless they run into a problem and need to call on him. See Wikipedia, s.v. "Moralistic Therapeutic Deism," accessed June 4, 2023, https://en.wikipedia.org/wiki/Moralistic _therapeutic_deism.

40. An example is the Canons of Dort, a Reformed confession. See "The Canons of Dort," Christian Reformed Church, accessed June 4, 2023, https://www.crcna.org/welcome/beliefs/confessions /canons-dort.

41. Joseph Chamie, "The End of Marriage in America?" The Hill, August 10, 2021, https://thehill.com/opinion/finance/567107 -the-end-of-marriage-in-america/.

42. Lydia Anderson, Zachary Scherer, "See How Marriage and Divorce Rates in Your State Stack Up," United States Census Bureau, December 7, 2020, https://www.census.gov/library /stories/2020/12/united-states-marriage-and-divorce-rates -declined-last-10-years.html.

43. Melissa Kearney, Phillip Levine, Luke Pardue, "The Mystery of the Declining U.S. Birth Rate," Econofact, February 15, 2022, https://econofact.org/the-mystery-of-the-declining-u-s-birth -rate.

44. "Unmarried Childbearing," Centers for Disease Control and Prevention, last reviewed January 31, 2023, https://www.cdc .gov/nchs/fastats/unmarried-childbearing.htm.

45. Emily Witt, "A Hookup App for the Emotionally Mature," *New Yorker*, July 11, 2022, https://www.newyorker.com /culture/annals-of-inquiry/feeld-dating-app-sex.

46. Terry Goodrich, "Evangelicals Have Higher-Than-Average Divorce Rates, According to a Report Compiled by Baylor for the Council on Contemporary Families," Baylor University, February 5, 2014, https://news.web.baylor.edu/news/story/2014 /evangelicals-have-higher-average-divorce-rates-according -report-compiled-baylor.

47. Michael Chancellor, "The Ongoing Epidemic of Pornography in the Church," Baptist News Global, January 27, 2021, https://baptistnews.com/article/the-ongoing-epidemic-of -pornography-in-the-church/.

48. According to Barna, 96 percent of pastors are married, and 96 percent of married pastors say their relationship with their spouse is good or excellent. See "How Healthy Are Pastors' Relationships?," Barna, February 15, 2017, https://www.barna .com/research/healthy-pastors-relationships/.

49. Brendan Case, Ying Chen, "For Long-Term Health and Happiness, Marriage Still Matters," *Wall Street Journal*,

March 18, 2023, https://www.wsj.com/articles/for-long-term
-health-and-happiness-marriage-still-matters-86114ced.

50. More than half the adult population is now single. See "Singles
Nation: Why Americans Are Turning Away from Marriage,"
WNYC Studios, September 11, 2014, https://www.wnycstudios
.org/podcasts/takeaway/segments/more-half-americans-are
-single. The number of single-person households has doubled
since 1980. See Harry Bruinius, "Party of One: Why Record
Numbers of Americans Are Going It Alone," Christian Science
Monitor, December 13, 2021, https://www.csmonitor.com
/USA/Society/2021/1213/Party-of-one-Why-record-numbers
-of-Americans-are-going-it-alone.

51. Jessica Bryant, "Women Continue to Outnumber Men in
College Completion," Best Colleges, July 8, 2022, https://www
.bestcolleges.com/news/analysis/2021/11/19/women-complete
-college-more-than-men/.

52. I would also argue that the mission of the church is more than
just a ministry to the unconverted.

CHAPTER 9: PURSUE OWNERSHIP

1. As we discussed in chapter 6.

2. These are predominantly nonprofit and thus not owned in a
legal sense, but in the nonprofit world, control of the board of
directors is typically tantamount to ownership.

3. Byrne Hobart, "The Payback Protection Plan," The Diff, https://
diff.substack.com/p/the-paycheck-protection-plan-where.

4. You can sign up for my newsletter at aaronrenn.com.

5. TBS, "Seinfeld: Ribbon (Clip)," YouTube, July 1, 2014, https://
www.youtube.com/watch?v=y4bmGekgE14.

6. "Our Story," General American Donut Company, https://
web.archive.org/web/20220602183450/https://www
.generalamerican.me/our-story.

7. Nassim Taleb, *Antifragile: Things That Gain from Disorder*,
Incerto (New York: Random House, 2014), 52.

8. Information about Maddox was sourced from interviews

with its CEO, Camden Spiller. All quotations are from author interviews.

9. "Company Profile: No.1,955, Maddox Industrial Transformer," Inc., accessed June 4, 2023, https://www.inc.com/profile/maddox-industrial-transformer.

10. Mark D. DeYmaz and Harry Li, *The Coming Revolution in Church Economics: Why Tithes and Offerings Are No Longer Enough, and What You Can Do About It* (Grand Rapids: Baker, 2019).

11. "For Suburban Texas Men, a Workout Craze with a Side of Faith," *New York Times*, September 24, 2022, https://www.nytimes.com/2022/09/24/us/f3-workout-men-texas.html.

12. The college is New St. Andrews. The media company is Canon Press. The coffee shop is Bucer's Coffeehouse Pub. And the gastropub is Tapped.

CHAPTER 10: BE A LIGHT

1. Anne Case and Angus Deaton, *Deaths of Despair and the Future of Capitalism* (Princeton, NJ: Princeton University Press, 2021).

2. "'A Decade of Fruitless Searching': The Toll of Dating App Burnout," *New York Times*, August 31, 2022, https://www.nytimes.com/2022/08/31/well/mind/burnout-online-dating-apps.html.

3. Mark Jobe, "New Life Cities: Urban Church," Vimeo, accessed June 5, 2023, https://vimeo.com/67468542.

4. Leonardo De Chirico, "Post-Christianity Is an Opportunity for Real Christianity," The Gospel Coalition, July 13, 2020, https://www.thegospelcoalition.org/reviews/post-christianity/.

5. He Gets Us, https://hegetsus.com/en.

6. Bob Smietana, "'He Gets Us' Organizers Hope to Spend $1 Billion to Promote Jesus. Will Anyone Care?," *Washington Post*, February 3, 2023, https://www.washingtonpost.com/religion/2023/02/03/he-gets-us-organizers-hope-spend-1-billion-promote-jesus-will-anyone-care/.

7. Cornerstone Television, "Talking 'He Gets Us' Ad Campaign with Bill McKendry | Hope Today," YouTube, April 13, 2022, https://www.youtube.com/watch?v=6MsHrBgzrQw.

8. As an example, see "He Gets Us Campaign Doesn't Get Jesus, Conservatives Say," Capstone Report, October 13, 2022, https://capstonereport.com/2022/10/13/he-gets-us-campaign-doesnt-get-jesus-conservatives-say/39511/.

9. After the 2023 NFL Super Bowl broadcast included ads from He Gets Us, multiple media outlets ran articles criticizing the campaign because the backers were said to be anti-LGBT and anti-abortion. See, for example, CNN at AJ Willingham, "The truth behind the 'He Gets Us' ads for Jesus airing during the Super Bowl," CNN, February 13, 2023, https://www.cnn.com/2023/02/11/us/he-gets-us-super-bowl-commercials-cec/index.html.

10. Moore wrote, "Bible Belt near-Christianity is teetering. I say let it fall." "Is Christianity Dying?" Russell Moore, May 12, 2015, https://www.russellmoore.com/2015/05/12/is-christianity-dying/.

11. In a since-deleted tweet, Ortlund said, "I rejoice at the decline of Bible Belt Religion." See https://web.archive.org/web/20210416175129/https://twitter.com/rayortlund/status/1381776675780841475.

12. A large number of Christian anti-addiction ministries exist, but one of the most famous is Teen Challenge (now Adult & Teen Challenge), founded by David Wilkerson, author of *The Cross and the Switchblade* (New York: Berkley, 1986). See https://teenchallengeusa.org/.

13. Caitlin Flanagan, "Losing the *Rare* in 'Safe, Legal, and Rare,'" *Atlantic*, December 6, 2019, https://www.theatlantic.com/ideas/archive/2019/12/the-brilliance-of-safe-legal-and-rare/603151/.

14. https://shoutyourabortion.com/.

15. Arianne Shahvisi, "What's the Difference?" *London Review of Books*, September 8, 2022, https://www.lrb.co.uk/the-paper/v44/n17/arianne-shahvisi/what-s-the-difference. Some people are intersex or have chromosomal anomalies. A very

small number of people also legitimately experience some type of gender dysphoria. But these claims about gender go well beyond this limited number of cases.

16. Alia E. Dastagir, "Marsha Blackburn Asked Ketanji Brown Jackson to Define 'Woman.' Science Says There's No Simple Answer," *USA Today*, March 27, 2022, https://www.usatoday.com/story/life/health-wellness/2022/03/24/marsha-blackburn-asked-ketanji-jackson-define-woman-science/7152439001/.

17. Romans 1:20 and 2:14. There are many ways to define natural law, but in the broadest sense we're talking about truth that corresponds to created reality.

18. James R. Wood, "Sheep, Wolves, and Fools," American Reformer, October 4, 2022, https://americanreformer.org/2022/10/sheep-wolves-and-fools/.

19. Wood, "Sheep, Wolves, and Fools."

20. Jen Hatmaker, Instagram, October 10, 2022, https://www.instagram.com/p/Cjik2RHMZkT/.

21. Emily Matchar, "Why I Can't Stop Reading Mormon Housewife Blogs," Salon, September 25, 2011, https://www.salon.com/2011/01/15/feminist_obsessed_with_mormon_blogs/.

22. Aaron Blake, "Mike Pence Doesn't Dine Alone with Other Women. And We're All Shocked," *Washington Post*, March 30, 2017, https://www.washingtonpost.com/news/the-fix/wp/2017/03/30/mike-pence-doesnt-dine-alone-with-other-women-and-were-all-shocked/.

23. Incel is short for "involuntarily celibate," both a description of a condition and the name of an online men's movement.

24. Wikipedia, s.v. "Letters of Julian/Letter 22," last edited December 10, 2012, https://en.wikisource.org/wiki/Letters_of_Julian/Letter_22.

25. "You asked, we answered: Why didn't any Wall Street CEOs go to jail after the financial crisis? It's complicated," MarketPlace, accessed June 5, 2023, https://features.marketplace.org/why-no-ceo-went-jail-after-financial-crisis/.

26. Wikipedia, s.v. "Wells Fargo Cross-Selling Scandal," Wikipedia, accessed June 5, 2023, https://en.wikipedia.org /wiki/Wells_Fargo_account_fraud_scandal.

27. "The Cash Monster Was Insatiable: How Insurers Exploited Medicare for Billions," *New York Times*, August 10, 2022, https://www.nytimes.com/2022/10/08/upshot/medicare -advantage-fraud-allegations.html.

28. "They Were Entitled to Free Care. Hospitals Hounded Them to Pay," *New York Times*, September 24, 2022, https://www .nytimes.com/2022/09/24/business/nonprofit-hospitals-poor -patients.html.

29. James Meek, "Somerdale to Skarbimierz James Meek follows Cadbury to Poland," *London Review of Books*, April 2017, https://www.lrb.co.uk/v39/n08/james-meek/somerdale-to -skarbimierz.

30. Kalyeena Makortoff, "Discredit history: 10 years of Barclays scandals," *Guardian*, November 1, 2021, https://www .theguardian.com/business/2021/nov/01/discredit-history-10 -years-of-barclays-scandals.

CHAPTER 11: BE A SOURCE OF TRUTH

1. "Live Not by Lies," The Aleksandr Solzhenitsyn Center, originally published February 12, 1974, accessed June 5, 2023, https://www.solzhenitsyncenter.org/live-not-by-lies.

2. John Bacon, "'Seriously people—STOP BUYING MASKS!': Surgeon general says they won't protect from coronavirus," The Florida Times-Union, March 2, 2020, https://www.jacksonville .com/story/news/healthcare/2020/03/02/seriously-people–stop -buying-masks-surgeon-general-says-they-wont-protect-from -coronavirus/112244966/.

3. Hunter Schwartz, "Obama's Latest 'Evolution' on Gay Marriage: He Lied about Opposing It," *Washington Post*, February 10, 2015, https://www.washingtonpost.com/news/the-fix/wp/2015 /02/10/axelrod-says-obama-lied-about-opposing-gay-marriage-its -another-convenient-evolution/.

4. See, for example, David Murrow, *Why Men Hate Going to Church* (Nashville: Thomas Nelson, 2011).

5. Multiple such attacks have taken place in Toronto alone. See "Teenage Boy Charged in Canada's First 'Incel' Terror Case," BBC News, May 20, 2020, https://www.bbc.com/news/world-us-canada-52733060.

6. Andrew Tate is one such figure. An estimated 80 percent of teenage boys in Britain have seen his content. See Maya Oppenheim, "Figures that lay bare the shocking scale of toxic influencer Andrew Tate's reach among young men," Independent, February 16, 2023, https://www.independent.co.uk/news/uk/home-news/andrew-tate-influence-young-men-misogyny-b2283595.html.

7. The egalitarian system is described in the book edited by Ronald W. Pierce et al., *Discovering Biblical Equality: Complementarity without Hierarchy* (Westmont, IL: IVP Academic, 2005).

8. Complementarianism is described in John Piper and Wayne Grudem, eds., *Recovering Biblical Manhood and Womanhood: A Response to Evangelical Feminism*, revised edition (Wheaton, IL: Crossway, 2021).

9. Interview with John Piper, "Should Women Be Police Officers?" Desiring God, accessed June 5, 2023, https://www.desiringgod.org/interviews/should-women-be-police-officers.

10. A simple Google search for "women initiate majority of divorces" will return an enormous number of references for this. See https://www.google.com/search?q=women+initiate+majority+of+divorces.

11. One example is gender differences in the "big five" personality traits. See Yanna Weisberg, Colin G. Deyoung, Jacob B. Hirsh, "Gender Differences in Personality across the Ten Aspects of the Big Five," ResearchGate, August 2011, https://www.researchgate.net/publication/51594567_Gender_Differences_in_Personality_across_the_Ten_Aspects_of_the_Big_Five.

12. Channel 4 News, "Jordan Peterson Debate on the Gender Pay

Gap, Campus Protests and Postmodernism," YouTube, January 16, 2018, https://www.youtube.com/watch?v=aMcjxSThD54.

13. Christian Rudder, "Men's Favorite Ages Are 20, 21, 22, and 23: A Data Dive by the Co-Founder of OKCupid," Jezebel, September 20, 2015, https://jezebel.com/mens-favorite-ages-are -20-21-22-and-23-a-data-dive-1731660984.

14. Robert Allison, "How Do Men Rate Women on Dating Websites? (Part 2)," SAS, October 16, 2014, https://blogs.sas .com/content/sastraining/2014/10/16/how-do-men-rate-women -on-dating-websites-part-2/.

15. Worst Online Dater, "Tinder Experiments II: Guys, unless you are really hot you are probably better off not wasting your time on Tinder—a quantitative socio-economic study," Medium, March 24, 2015, https://medium.com/@worstonlinedater /tinder-experiments-ii-guys-unless-you-are-really-hot-you-are -probably-better-off-not-wasting-your-2ddf370a6e9a.

16. Timothy Keller with Kathy Keller, *The Meaning of Marriage*, 179–80.

17. There are some examples, obviously. But these are often from less prominent pastors whose work comes to broad attention only when it goes viral after accusations of sexism, such as with the example of pastor Stewart-Allen Clark in Missouri. See Elisha Fieldstadt, "Missouri pastor on leave after sexist sermon preaching wives need to look good for their husbands," NBC News, March 8, 2021, https://www.nbcnews.com/news /us-news/missouri-pastor-leave-after-sexist-sermon-preaching -wives-need-look-n1259998.

18. Tony Reinke, "10 Questions on Dating with Matt Chandler," Desiring God, February 14, 2015, https://www.desiringgod .org/articles/10-questions-on-dating-with-matt-chandler.

19. Jordan Peterson (@JordanpetersonInspire), Facebook video, December 18, 2022, https://www.facebook.com /Jordanpetersoninspire/videos/girls-arent-attracted-to -boys-who-are-their-friends-even-though-they-might-like -/921945898788154/.

20. Daniel J. Kruger, "Reproductive Strategies and Relationship Preferences Associated with Prestigious and Dominant Men," ResearchGate, February 2011, https://www.researchgate .net/publication/229277861_Reproductive_strategies_and _relationship_preferences_associated_with_prestigious_and _dominant_men.

21. "The 4 Sure Signs of Confidence Women Look for in a Man," eHarmony, October 11, 2011, https://www.eharmony.com /dating-advice/dating/the-4-sure-signs-of-confidence-women -look-for-in-a-man/.

22. As one example, most women are well known to prefer men taller than themselves. See John Malouff, "Why Do Women Tend to Prefer Tall Men?" Using Psychology, August 17, 2014, https://blog.une.edu.au/usingpsychology/2014/08/17/why-do -women-tend-to-prefer-tall-men/.

23. David J. Ayers, "Doomed to Marry beneath Them? Marriage and the Gender Gap in College Education," Christian Post, October 11, 2021, https://www.christianpost.com/voices /doomed-to-marry-beneath-them-marriage-and-the-gender-gap .html.

24. Robinson Meyer, "Dude, She's (Exactly 25 Percent) Out of Your League," *Atlantic,* August 10, 2018, https://www .theatlantic.com/science/archive/2018/08/online-dating-out -of-your-league/567083/.

25. Russell Moore describes some of this emerging pressure. See Russell Moore, "Let's Rethink the Evangelical Gender Wars," *Christianity Today*, February 13, 2023, https://www .christianitytoday.com/ct/2023/march/lets-rethink-evangelical -gender-wars.html.

26. Aja Romano, "Harry Potter and the Author Who Failed Us," Vox, June 11, 2020, https://www.vox.com/culture/21285396/jk -rowling-transphobic-backlash-harry-potter.

27. "Meaning of Kephale after 30 Years," Wayne Grudem, accessed June 5, 2023, http://www.waynegrudem.com/meaning -of-kephale-after-30-years.

28. Their statement of principles is known as the Danvers Statement. The book is the previously mentioned *Recovering Biblical Manhood and Womanhood.*

29. This is easy to see in the original complementarian manifesto, known as "The Danvers Statement," The Council on Biblical Manhood and Womanhood, accessed June 5, 2023, https://cbmw.org/about/danvers-statement/.

30. John Piper and Wayne Grudem, eds., *Recovering Biblical Manhood and Womanhood: A Response to Evangelical Feminism*, rev. edition (Wheaton, IL: Crossway, 2021).

31. "The Danvers Statement," The Council on Biblical Manhood and Womanhood, accessed June 7, 2023, https://cbmw.org/about/danvers-statement/.

32. James Davison Hunter, *Evangelicalism: The Coming Generation* (Chicago: The University of Chicago Press, 1987), 96–97, 104.

33. Hunter, *Evangelicalism*, 103–105.

34. Tim Keller is widely viewed as an expounder of third way positions. William McMillan, who wrote his doctoral dissertation at Yale on Redeemer Presbyterian Church, wrote, "Keller seems to enjoy presenting Christianity as the third way: the way that keeps one on the straight and narrow; that keeps one from veering into the ditch on the right or the one on the left." See William M. McMillan, "Contextualization, Big Apple Style: Making Conservative Christianity More Palatable in Modern Day Manhattan," Yale University, accessed June 5, 2023, https://symposia.library.utoronto.ca/index.php/symposia/article/download/19800/16814/48445.

35. The Gospel Coalition, "How to Understand Biblical Complementarianism," YouTube, September 23, 2022, https://www.youtube.com/watch?v=jyjkAMeBtto.

36. In cases of divorce, there has been a shift toward joint custody, though this remains the minority position for now. Also, 40 percent of births today are out of wedlock, and unmarried fathers have significant problems asserting parental rights. As Brookings Institution scholar Richard Reeves notes in his book

Of Boys and Men, "In every U.S. state, an unmarried mother is the presumed sole custodial parent. Unmarried fathers must first prove paternity (in married couples this is assumed), and then petition for visitation and custody. For many fathers this can prove a difficult process. In the meantime, the mother can choose to bar all access. Regardless of visitation rights, however, unmarried fathers will typically be obliged to pay child support, often at levels that low-income fathers in particular struggle to meet." See: https://www.demographic -research.org/volumes/vol46/38/46-38.pdf, and Reeves, *Of Boys and Men*, 215.

37. Reeves also notes, "Mothers have also received growing support from the welfare system, allowing even those with low or no earnings to be freer of the need for a breadwinning husband." Reeves, *Of Boys and Men*, 55.

38. In a study of sermons discussing divorce, feminist scholar Valerie Hobbs found, "In summary, despite the fact that femaleness was, as mentioned earlier, a significant semantic concept in the divorce corpus, women are framed primarily as receivers of divorce rather than initiators. Although in most cases of divorce in the United States, women initiate divorce, pastors in the corpus in this way represented divorce as a largely male action." See Hobbs, "The Discourse of Divorce in Conservative Christian Sermons," *Critical Discourse Studies* 17, no. 2 (2020): 193–210, https://doi.org/10.1080 /17405904.2019.1665079.

39. An example is John Moody, coauthor of John Moody and Joel Salatin, *The Frugal Homesteader: Living the Good Life on Less* (Vancouver: New Society Publishers, 2018) and graduate of Southern Baptist Theological Seminary. See https:// johnwmoody.com/.

40. An example is Eric Brende, who runs an artisanal soap-making business and has sought to detach himself from the industrial economy in an urban context. See Eric Brende, "How to Beat the High Cost of Working," *Wall Street Journal*, August 31,

2018, https://www.wsj.com/articles/how-to-beat-the-high-cost
-of-working-1535747253.

41. An example is Douglas Wilson. See Douglas Wilson, "The Lie
of Servant Leadership," Blog and Mablog, March 11, 2020,
https://dougwils.com/books-and-culture/s7-engaging-the
-culture/the-lie-of-servant-leadership.html.

42. David Talcott, "Man and Woman in Christ: 40 Years Later,"
The Council on Biblical Manhood and Womanhood, June 8,
2019, https://cbmw.org/2019/06/08/man-and-woman-in-christ
-40-years-later/.

43. Aaron Renn, "Jordan Peterson's Folk Wisdom," Mere
Orthodoxy, April 9, 2018, https://mereorthodoxy.com/jordan
-petersons-folk-wisdom/.

CHAPTER 12: BE PRUDENTIALLY ENGAGED

1. Russell Moore, "Christian Nationalism Cannot Save the
World," *Christianity Today*, September 29, 2022, https://www
.christianitytoday.com/ct/2022/september-web-only/christian
-nationalism-cannot-save-world-politics-elections.html.

2. Emily Brindley, "Critical Race Theory Debate Is Tearing Apart
the Christian Church, Fort Worth Pastors Say," Fort Worth Star-
Telegram, updated July 23, 2021, https://www.star
-telegram.com/news/politics-government/article252897943.html.

3. For example, Hillary Clinton participated in attempting to
discredit women who had credibly accused her husband of
sexual misconduct. See, "90s Scandals Threaten to Erode
Hillary Clinton's Strength with Women," *New York Times*,
January 21, 2016, https://www.nytimes.com/2016/01/21/us
/politics/90s-scandals-threaten-to-erode-hillary-clintons
-strength-with-women.html.

4. Scott Sauls, Twitter, October 8, 2022, https://twitter.com
/scottsauls/status/1578868000916004864.

5. James Davison Hunter, *To Change the World: The Irony,
Tragedy, and Possibility of Christianity in the Late Modern
World* (Oxford: Oxford University Press, 2010).

6. Alan Jacobs, "When Character No Longer Counts," National Affairs, Spring 2017, https://www.nationalaffairs.com /publications/detail/when-character-no-longer-counts.

7. Rob Dreher, "What I Saw at the Jericho March," The American Conservative, December 12, 2020, https://www .theamericanconservative.com/what-i-saw-at-the-jericho -march/.

8. See, for example, Scott Klusendorf, "The 2012 Elections: Five Questions for Pro-Life Advocates," Christian Research Institute, updated July 31, 2022, https://www.equip.org /articles/the-2012-elections-five-questions-for-pro-life -advocates/.

9. Julius Krein, "The Value of Nothing: Capital versus Growth," American Affairs, Fall 2021, https://americanaffairsjournal .org/2021/08/the-value-of-nothing-capital-versus-growth/.

10. Carol Hanisch, "The Women's Liberation Movement classic with a new explanatory introduction," Carol Hanisch, accessed June 5, 2023, https://www.carolhanisch.org /CHwritings/PIP.html.

11. Ed Feulner, "Government Intrudes into Virtually Every Aspect of Our Lives," *Daily Signal*, January 5, 2014, https://www .dailysignal.com/2014/01/05/alarming-growth-government/.

12. Michael Wear, who previously worked in President Obama's Office of Faith-based and Neighborhood Partnerships, is an example of an evangelical who is a Democrat. See Mark Silk, "Obama Campaign Taps Young Adviser, Michael Wear, for Faith Outreach," Religion News Service, May 14, 2012, https://religionnews.com/2012/05/14/obama-campaign-taps -young-adviser-for-faith-outreach/.

13. These sources, among other things, pre-date the rise of mass media and social media, which have profoundly changed how society functions. See books such as Walter Lippmann's *Public Opinion*, Edward Herman and Noam Chomsky's *Manufacturing Consent*, Jacques Ellul's *Propaganda*, and Neil Postman's *Amusing Ourselves to Death*.

CONCLUSION

1. Rod Dreher, "The Final Christian Generation?," The American Conservative, December 23, 2020, https://www .theamericanconservative.com/final-christian-generation -jeremiah/.

2. Office of International Religious Freedom, "2020 Report on International Religious Freedom: Egypt," U.S. Department of State, May 12, 2021, https://www.state.gov/reports/2020 -report-on-international-religious-freedom/egypt/.

3. Walter Kaegi, "Egypt on the eve of the Muslim conquest," Cambridge University Press, March 28, 2008, https:// www.cambridge.org/core/books/abs/cambridge-history -of-egypt/egypt-on-the-eve-of-the-muslim-conquest /AD46F69B805C49FA770BD9B2FB4B45AC#.

4. Steven Viney, "Who Are Egypt's Coptic Christians and Why Are They Persecuted?," ABC News, April 8, 2017, https://www .abc.net.au/news/2017-04-10/who-are-egypts-copts/8429634.

5. The recent Asbury University revival in early 2023 prompted renewed discussions of spiritual awakenings, with Russell Moore saying it "reminds us that God works in ways we cannot control." See Russell Moore, "Celebrating Revival in a Cynical Age," Christianity Today, February 23, 2023, https:// www.christianitytoday.com/ct/2023/february-web-only/russell -moore-ct-asbury-revival-charismatic-cynical-age.html.